Early praise for *Read 'Em & Reap*:

"Whether you read for work or for fun, this powerful little book will affirm the benefits ... of both! Because of *Read 'Em & Reap*, I'm reading more these days and feeling less guilty about reading for leisure/escape. How's that for impact?!"

– Sybil Stershic, author of *Taking Care of the People Who Matter Most* and *Share of Heart, Share of Mind*

"Spectacular news! This book will help you to re-frame the time you spend reading ... strategically to help keep you in tip-top cognitive shape. *Read 'Em and Reap* will show you not only why reading helps you live longer, but what to read, and how to read so you can benefit from the longevity effect regular reading delivers."

– Pamela Wilson, author of *Master Content Marketing* and *Master Content Strategy*

"*Read 'Em & Reap*: impactful, empirical, and inspirational are just three adjectives I'd use to describe Tom Collins' new book. Tom has achieved a delicate balance of "educating with elegance," and I highly recommend this book ... it might wean you off the iPad, after all."

– James Sugarman, co-founder, 4GenNow intergenerational entrepreneurship organization

"Brilliant! The whole concept of *Read 'Em & Reap* is so needed. I truly appreciate the intelligent nudge it's given me to make more time to read!"

– Mia Voss - *Mia On The Go*, Storyteller
Luxury Travel & Lifestyle Writer
Brand Promoter & Speaker

"*Read 'Em & Reap* is an important reminder of the many benefits of reading, as well a helpful introduction to the love of reading for those who haven't yet engaged with books. Part of its value comes from being a short, easy to read treatment, yet I found myself reacting to several research revelations with variations of, 'Cool! I didn't know this ...'

"This book will inspire others, as it has me, to read more and would make a wonderful introductory book for those new to book clubs, starting high school or college, embarking on career learning programs, etc. With all the things people do to improve and extend their lives, it's great that reading is one and, hey, it might even motivate you to a better diet and more exercise!"

– David Gower, Founder, New Clean Earth, LLC and Youbicwitus™

"It's no surprise to me that Tom Collins has written *Read 'Em & Reap*. From our many conversations over the years, he's simply the right person at the right time. ... There is so much in the book to commend it, reminders for all the reasons to read, leading to Tom's call to 'Take Action' – which may lead you to friends old and new, vibrant conversations, and as in my case, feeling compelled to write!"

– Bruce Peters, entrepreneurial guide and founder of Beyond Teal: Transform Life at Work™

"Bravo! *Read 'Em & Reap* is a winner! I'll be sharing it."

– Shawna Schuh - *Ignite* executive coaching, speaker, and author of *51 Ways to Pick Up Your Get-Up-And-Go*

Read 'Em & Reap

6 Science-Backed Ways Reading Puts You on the Road to Achieving More and *Living* Longer

Tom Collins

WME Books
imprint of
Old Dog Digital, LLC
Binghamton, NY, USA

Read 'Em & Reap
Copyright © 2019 by Tom Collins

ISBN: 978-1-934229-36-1

Published in USA by Old Dog Digital, LLC, Binghamton, NY
     under its WME Books imprint

Editor: Yvonne DiVita
Interior & Cover Designer: Tom Collins

For special orders and bulk discounts contact:
     tom@OldDogLearning.com

Disclaimers:

While the author and publisher have used their best efforts in preparing this book, they make no representations or warranties regarding the accuracy or completeness of the contents of this book or any related, referenced, or linked materials. The author and publisher specifically disclaim any implied warranties of merchantability or fitness for a particular purpose, and make no guarantees whatsoever that you will achieve any particular result.

We believe all information, scientific research, and case studies and results persented herein are true and accurate, but we have not independently audited or confirmed the research methods, data collection, or results reported. Any advice or strategies contained in this book might not even be suitable for your situation and you should consult your own advisors as appropriate.

For Yvonne, whose love, support, and inspiration make everything both possible and worth it.

Gratitudes

"I just want to thank everybody who made this day necessary."

— Yogi Berra

As many have lamented, it's not possible to thank everybody who deserves my gratitude, not even if I try to focus only on those who influenced this book. I do recognize the irony that my own thesis on the impact of reading means I owe thanks to a significant swath of humanity over the last 6,000 years or so.

Apologies to all those I'm inevitably omitting. For those still living, let's (re)connect and I can thank you in person or online. I'll set up a page on my blog for you to leave a comment and we can go from there.

Here, I'll start with thanks to my dear friend and mentor, Bruce Peters, whose deeply satisfying conversations and probing questions over many years helped make the writing of this book **necessary**. He knows what we mean by necessary! And to Lee Thayer, who added that nuance to our lexicon.

To Pamela Wilson for all she's taught me about design and business over the years; for the link share on Facebook that turned this idea into a project; for her feedback that forced me to rethink and rewrite what are now Chapters 7-9; and for her Foreword.

To Sybil Stershic, James Sugarman, David Gower, Mia Voss, Dino Dogan, Brenda Lidestri, and Shawna Schuh, for reading and critiquing early drafts. Their contributions to making this book more readable and more useful are immense. All it's remaining faults are mine alone. My only excuse is knowing that at some point you have to stop and "let the baby be born" and this was my judgment.

To the authors of all the books I've read, especially those cited directly in this one. I'll simply call out Katie Myers, Kimberly Alexander, Anastasia Button, Erika Armstrong, and Eric Meade as authors I got to meet personally while we lived in Colorado, whose vibrant spirits and the books they published helped inspire me to get this one done!

I'll amend the thanks to the authors of all the books I've read or cited. No, to the authors of all the books. Period. To understand why, skip to the Conclusion and find the quote I shared from Galileo. Then turn that page to my Marvel-esque "extra" scene.

To my family and the blended one I now share with Yvonne. You'll see more in the Introduction how my Mom drove my earliest reading. And my Dad instilled my DIY-er mentality that pretty much any problem is "figure-out-able" with the right manual.

To my two kids, Brendan and Elizabeth, whose insatiable curiosity kept me on my toes and made life-long learning necessary for me, too.

And to Yvonne's three, Chloe, Maggie, and Don, who accepted me into their lives and inspired me with their varied approaches, stimulating talks, and occasionally challenges to my own thinking – always a valuable gift.

To Yvonne . . . well, she's here by my side and there aren't enough trees left to thank her properly in print, so I'll just have to try my best to show her.

Contents

Dedication – vii

Gratitudes – ix

Foreword – xv

Preface: on Deep Reading (and "MWe") – 1
Deep reading as an interactive process – 2
The mind we share – 5
My side of MWe – 8
CUE your side of this synapse – 11

Introduction – 13
Readers are … – 15
Your brain on books (and your body, too) – 16

Ch. 1 - Reading Reduces Stress – 19
A double-edged sword – 19
Reducing negative stress
helps more than our careers – 22
Reaping the stress-reducing rewards of reading – 24
Fact or fiction? – 25

Ch. 2 - Helps You Sleep – 29
More than physical restoration – 31
What's reading got to do with sleep? – 33

Ch. 3 - Improves Your Decision-Making Capacity – 35
Reading grows your brain – 36
Acquiring "the Knowledge" – 37
Two side notes on growing your brain through learning – 40
Fiction increases perspective, comprehension, and readiness to take action – 41
Building your "reading brain circuit" – 42

Ch. 4 - Makes You a Better Leader – 45
Empathy as a core leadership skill – 47
Read, that's an order! – 52

Ch. 5 - Makes You Smarter – 53
The more you read, the more you know – 54
Reading improves your brain's processing power, too – 56

Ch. 6 - Helps You Live Longer – 61
How much longer? – 62
The future is already here – 63
How reading helps you live longer – 67
Reading as a life multiplier – 69

Ch. 7 - Print or Digital – 71
Some advantages of print – 72
Music to your eyes – 74
Some downsides of digital – 77
Remedial reading? – 79

Ch. 8 - Adopt Your Own Reading Plan – 81

3 tips for adding more
reading to your life – 85

Bonus tip:
Subscribe, strategically – 89

Ch. 9 - Take Action – 93

Conclusion: As You Read – 101

Indexed References – 109

Foreword

Want to live longer?

"Alternate between an hour of aerobic exercise and an hour of strength training every day."

"Sleep at least eight hours every night."

"Eat eight portions of vegetables and five portions of fruit every day." "Eat red meat." "Follow a plant-based diet."

Actually ... "Don't eat at all – fast."

When it comes to longevity advice, we have heard it all. Sometimes the same "live longer tips" we heard just last year are contradicted by this year's newest study.

That's why, when Tom Collins mentioned a habit I already cherish – reading – might actually help me live longer, I was delighted.

For those of us who already love to read, this is spectacular news. This book will help you to re-frame the time you spend reading not as passive downtime, but rather active "uptime" you're using strategically to help keep you in tip-top cognitive shape.

If you're someone who enjoys reading but lacks motivation to do it regularly, this book will light a fire under you to schedule regular reading time and stick to it.

If you've ever wondered whether reading print or digital made a difference, you'll find some answers in these pages. And if you've wondered whether your entertainment or sports magazine was going to help boost your brainpower, you'll find that answer, too (but you may not like it!).

All in all, *Read 'Em and Reap* will show you not only *why* reading helps you live longer, but *what* to read, and *how* to read so you can benefit from the longevity effect regular reading delivers.

Here's to a long, healthy, word-filled future!

— Pamela Wilson
Founder, BIG Brand System
Nashville, TN | March, 2019

Preface: on Deep Reading (and "MWe")

> *"Deep reading ... is a process of inquiry built around the exploration of 'challenging questions' and 'troublesome knowledge.'"*
> — Patrick Sullivan

> *"We are an inherently collaborative species ... collaboration is at the heart of what **MWe** can do ...."*
> — Dr. Daniel J. Siegel

You'll find the term "deep reading" mentioned throughout this book. In fact, for you to enjoy many of the benefits of reading we'll be exploring, the science suggests that deep reading is key.

When I ran into the term in my research, I felt I understood it and you would, too. But then, readers of earlier drafts posed one of those "challenging questions" to me:

What do we really mean by deep reading?

Deep reading as an interactive process

Turns out to be more complicated than I thought, as well as a controversial topic in academic and political circles. I'm not going to delve into the politics here and will touch on the academic disputes only to note two main approaches to reading that you might think of when you see the term deep reading.

One is labeled "close reading," where the reader carefully examines a text to find its main points, themes, or ideas, and identify the arguments, evidence, or narrative that supports or conveys the meaning. This approach assumes there is a single, objectively discoverable meaning in the text itself, resulting in the one right answer that standardized testing depends on.

Critics decry this as an "answer-getting disposition," where the reader is extracting a fixed meaning from the text.

Even critics of answer-getting agree that close reading is a useful part of a reader's skillset. But they object to stopping there, to limiting the role of the reader to a passive recipient of meaning.

The second approach ascribes to readers a "problem-exploring disposition" and more fully captures what I mean using the term "deep reading." This approach treats the reader as an active participant in constructing meaning from text. In *Deep Reading: Teaching Reading in the Writing Classroom,* the editors build on Louise Rosenblatt's theory of reading as

> "an event in the life of a reader, as a doing, a making, a combustion fed by the coming together of a particular personality and a particular text at a particular time."

This "coming together" is unique to each reader and inherently differs over time or context. With a problem-exploring disposition, readers generate meanings from

> "curiosity, reflection, consideration of multiple possibilities, a willingness to engage in a recursive process of trial and error, and ... a recognition that more than one solution can 'work.'"

Marcel Proust helped us see how writer and reader work together **through** a text to construct meanings:

> "Indeed, this is one of the great and wondrous characteristics of beautiful books ... for the author they may be called Conclusions, but for the reader, Provocations. We can feel that our wisdom begins where the author's ends, and we want him to give us answers when all he can do is give us desires. ... [B]y a strange law ... we cannot receive truth from anyone else, ... we must create it ourselves."

> *"... our wisdom begins where the author's ends"*

Note that this formulation of deep reading as active involvement by readers in creating meaning and producing knowledge applies to all types of writing:

- Hawking to Hemingway
- Aristotle to Asimov
- King (Carole) to King (Stephen) to King (Martin Luther)
- Shakespeare to Seuss

I purposely ended this list with Dr. Seuss. I want to presage my call later on, urging you to pass on both the love and the ability for future generations to engage in deep reading. You'll learn why the "deep reading circuits" in our brains are not hard-wired at birth, but must be nurtured in our kids.

On that point, my research uncovered a helpful book on teaching deep reading, *What Readers Really Do: Teaching the Process of Meaning Making*. Not only is it filled with tips for bringing deep reading skills to students, but one chapter title nicely connects the how of deep reading to the writing process:

*How Readers Draft and Revise
Their Way from Confusion to Clarity*

We'll return to this connection later. But consider this draft-revise approach to working with authors through the books you read. Can their imagined characters pose the "challenging questions" or their researched insights and arguments offer up the sort of "troublesome knowledge" that deep reading addresses? Will drafting and revising your understandings from the text as you read connect your wisdom to the author's? Will you construct new meanings together?

Will MWe?

The mind we share

The term "MWe" comes from Daniel Siegel's *Mind: A Journey to the Heart of Being Human*. His exploratory journey ranges across many scientific fields including neurobiology, anthropology, quantum physics, and complex systems theory. He carefully builds his case for concluding that our minds are more than enskulled brain activity, more than embodied nervous system impulses flowing within us.

Incorporating both these enskulled and embodied aspects, he proposes a broader working definition of mind as:

> "an embodied and relational
> process that regulates the flow
> of energy and information."

Connecting his relational view of mind to deep reading (without using that term), Siegel explains that

> "this view embraces the interactive ways in which both other people **and the artifacts they create** move the mind beyond the interior of the individual ... 'into the material world and into the social world' ..."

He also makes clear that these "artifacts" include books, repeatedly using phrases like "as I write and you read these words" to converse with his readers **through** his book.

This concept of a social or distributed mind and its connection to reading is not new to Siegel. Another place it appears that inspires my call for intergenerational reading is in *Thirty Million Words: Building a Child's Brain*. In a chapter on neuroplasticity, the authors cite research showing the need for human interaction, not merely exposure through audio or video devices, in the acquisition of language.

> "The brain may be brilliant, but ... it's a social creature. ... It does not learn language passively, but only in an environment of social responsiveness and social interaction."

Connecting this to reading and, indeed, to learning in general, they note:

> "[C]hildren begin school by learning to read with the ultimate goal of **reading to learn**."

Their practical advice on how parents and adults should engage in an interactive reading process they call "book sharing" is founded on science showing how children benefit if they

> "take a more active role in telling the story, including asking questions

and talking about what they see, think, and feel."

Deep reading from day one, eh? Another aspect of our relational mind.

To encapsulate his active and interactive relational mind, Siegel offers the pronoun **MWe**. It's a way to maintain as true the paradox of both our separate and our social selves.

> "*MWe* can be viewed as our integrated identity, the linkage of a differentiated *me* with a differentiated *we*, all in one integrated and integrating self."

Pulling together these ideas about deep reading and its relationship to writing, I've come to think of books as social synapses. Within us, a synapse fires when the sending neuron builds enough electro-chemical "action potential" to transmit a signal across the space between it and the receiving cell. When a writer puts enough potential into the words on the page and readers bring their own active participation close enough, sparks of meanings can come alive between.

I've come to think of books as social synapses.

Energy and information flow, both within and between us.

Which prompted me to move my version of an "About the Author" section here. If *mwe* are to construct meanings together, it may help to give you a glimpse of what's gone into forming the axons and dendrites on my side of the synapse.

My side of MWe

I think of reading as part of my compulsive "dot" collecting. I adapted that notion from a couple of ideas promoted by Steve Jobs.

In his famous 2005 commencement speech at Stanford, he touted the value of learning things that might not seem relevant to the students' current work or planned careers. He used the example of a calligraphy course he took after dropping out of college and suggested without that earlier experience, the Mac would not have featured beautiful typography.

Jobs emphasized the importance of accumulating diverse experiences over your lifetime to draw upon when needed, saying,

> "You can't connect the dots looking forward; you can only connect them looking backward."

In *Organizing Genius*, Warren Bennis picked up on another Jobs quote about creative people simply having accumulated more experiences, which they can connect to synthesize new ideas. Applied to Alan Kay, the leader of the personal computer team at Xerox PARC, Bennis wrote:

> "Exposed to art, music, and science from birth and a voracious and far-ranging **reader**, Kay had a vast number of experiential dots to connect."

Preface: On Deep Reading (and "MWe")

After 25 years practicing law, I built my first solo legal consulting practice around that theme and wrote about it in my inaugural blog post back in 2003. The tagline for that blog:

> "Thinking about how legal knowledge workers collect, and then connect, the dots."

My earlier experiences include Boy Scout leadership roles, high school team sports, car repair and maintenance, drum and bugle corps soloist, meat market clerk, swimming pool and backyard deck and patio construction, SLR photography and dark room work, youth soccer coaching, along with my more formal education through a B.A. in History, my J.D., and 31 credits toward a Masters in Informatics.

Just about every one of these jobs and roles involved reading.

When I was driving junkers that required serious maintenance work on most weekends, I kept the Chilton DIY manual for my current make and model in the trunk. When I was running pool installation crews, I quickly learned that every yard was a little different and kept the installation manual handy for rechecking how a certain step needed modification to fit the landscape. Music and marching showed me whole different languages and notation to learn and read.

This reading-biased approach to learning what I need to know to accomplish a task has not changed much. Most products arrive these days with a single sheet of instructions, often less than helpful. I've learned to hunt down more detailed versions online and read (or watch the video) there. And if the job is more complex, download them, and print out the sections I need to assemble, adjust, or repair the item in question (including still screen shots from the videos, with my own notes from the voice over).

Thus, my bookshelves now include an ever growing collection of DIY manuals, *Dummies*-style books, and folders of printed downloads. Topics range from construction trades to web-design to business and marketing to human development and neuro-science. Glancing around, I rediscovered books on camping skills, SCUBA diving, youth soccer, furniture finishing, and ... well, you might understand why our kids groan each time we move!

You'll see in several chapters how and why I've returned to reading fiction, as well. With all the benefits we'll cover, I'm most happy that writing this book gave that old and wonderful habit back to me. My default daily reading pattern has become non-fiction books, blogs, newsletters in the morning, fiction books in the evening. More on that in Chapter 2.

That should give you some idea of who I am and how I came to write this book. I'll be sharing other "experiential dots" I've gathered along the way, as we explore the benefits of reading. And you can take our deep reading, interactive learning further by connecting via the *Old Dog Learning* blogsite.

CUE your side of this synapse

Over to you. Of course I hope these pages will build enough potential for energy and information flow to set off sparks of meaning. But that depends equally on you.

Your "CUE" comes from *What Readers Really Do*. The reading process begins with **C**omprehension, described by the authors very similarly to the "answer-getting dispostion" of extracting a literal meaning from the text.

Calling this "the floor, not the ceiling, of meaning making," they urge us to continue to **U**nderstanding. This step involves

> "inferring on a larger scale, as readers recognize patterns and ... ***connect the dots*** of their line-by-line, page-by-page comprehension to help them see a bigger picture that may not have been apparent before."

And still, you won't be done. **E**valuation is

> "when readers take what they've come to understand about a text and consider its worth or merit, personally, intellectually, socially, or politically."

11

Indeed, the authors remind that the C-U-E process "isn't linear." You'll shift among them as you draft and revise your way toward clarity.

They point out that this draft and revise reading process often requires us to postpone our desire for clarity, as new ideas and more information are revealed. Thus, "we may find the answers if we **read on** attentively."

And they warn that

> "the process doesn't ever quite end. We continue to make meaning as ***texts live within us***, informing and coloring our lives, our choices, our opinions, even our actions."

That is my BHAG (big hairy audacious goal) for us: that this book will prompt you to new insight and understanding of how reading benefits your brain, body, and life. And that it will inspire you to take action.

I know this book will live on in me. Let's see if the potential energy and information flow it contains is enough to spark meaning for you.

Read on.

Introduction

> *"My secret weapon is that I read."*
>
> — Joan Westenberg

Mine was Donald Duck comic books. I learned to read and to love reading with that irascible Disney character, his troubles with the misadventures of Huey, Dewey, and Louie, Uncle Scrooge, and Daisy's way of smoothing things over.

Reflecting the longevity theme we'll focus on in Chapter 6, these characters have staying power. Donald is now an octogenarian, born in 1934 and still going strong since 2017 on the *DuckTales* TV cartoon series reboot.

Read 'Em & Reap — Tom Collins

When I was three my grandpa bought me a subscription to *Donald Duck* comics. My mom started out patiently reading them to me, but I can still remember struggling to sound out words myself and later running to the kitchen in frustration, demanding to know how some new word sounded or what it meant.

Uncle Scrooge with Huey, Louie, and Dewey; Panel from *"Return to Plain Awful"* by Don Rosa, 1989; Source: Wikipedia (see Indexed References)

By the time I started school, I was reading *Donald Duck*, *Archie*, and all the super hero issues that our local barber shop had on its table.

I've always described reading as something like an addiction – I'm simply unable to avoid reading. I read just about anything with English text that appears in my field of vision. Books, magazines, CNN screen tickers, milk cartons, cereal boxes, billboards, ads on benches, brick walls, and buses (inside and out), labels on shipping boxes, quotes on t-shirts, you name it.

So, what is it that makes reading a secret weapon?

Readers are . . .

You've probably heard the saying that *leaders are readers*, right?

Or maybe it's the other way around, *readers are leaders*? Harry Truman is supposed to have nixed that, quoted as saying, "Not all readers are leaders, but all leaders are readers."

Another version, usually attributed to female journalism pioneer Margaret Fuller, proposes this sequence and perhaps a causal relationship, "Today a reader, tomorrow a leader."

Whichever end they start from, such statements describing the benefits of reading in practical, career- and business-oriented terms. That limited focus continues in many articles and blog posts through the present.

Just a few recent titles:
- *Why Leaders Must Be Readers*, Forbes
- *For Those Who Want to Lead, Read*, Harvard Business Review
- *5 Ways Reading Makes You a Better Leader*, Michael Hyatt blog
- *4 Reasons Good Leaders Are Readers*, Jeremy Kingsley blog

- *5 Science-Backed Reasons Why Readers Do Better in Their Careers*, The Muse blog

However, I think this work-related mindset actually understates the benefits of reading. And the emerging science investigating how reading affects our brains, our emotions, and our overall health backs me up.

> *A work-related mindset **understates** the benefits of reading.*

Your brain on books (and your body, too)

The articles on reading listed above, use titles focusing on leadership and career advancement. But they point to scientific papers finding benefits that are **not** limited to our work lives. So let's dig into them a little deeper.

The first five chapters will build and expand on the points outlined in the *5 Science-Backed Reasons* article listed above. Plus, I'm adding a sixth reason uncovered in my own reading and research. The six are organized into chapters 1–6, as follows:

1. Reading Reduces Stress
2. Helps You Sleep
3. Improves Your Decision-Making Capacity
4. Makes You a Better Leader

5. Makes You Smarter

6. Helps You Live Longer

That last one might surprise you. It sure surprised me, when I first saw the headline connecting reading with living longer.

But when we get through the first five, I'm confident that #6 will fit in comfortably for you, too.

*Yes, reading even helps you **live** longer.*

During the writing, I decided to expand a section comparing how we read printed material (especially books) with scanning digital text across the many screens we all spend time looking at these days. That became chapter 7.

Chapter 8, offers specific suggestions on how you can adopt your own reading plan, or adapt your current reading habits, so that you can reap the rewards we'll be exploring together. Then in Chapter 9, I'll urge you to "take action" on your reading and pass the rewards on, with some steps you can apply at work and life.

I've worked really hard to keep this book as short as possible. My goal is to provide you with some compelling reasons to add more reading time, especially more books, to your busy life. Not have you spend it reading this one!

You may note the outside margins are a bit wider than usual. That's to encourage you to take notes, right here in the book. Yes, I hear some gasping about writing in a book. But you'll see why I favor that practice in my tips for expanding and improving your reading habits.

My title, of course, plays on the poker expression, though I hope I've avoided any hint of the smug "gotcha" tone often heard with, "Read 'em and weep." But I **am** confident that reading more will help you reap substantial benefits.

And some may surprise you.

So please do, read on.

* * * *

Note on references:

To minimize distractions in the text, you'll find a detailed list of books, research papers, and other references at the end of the book. I've indexed them to the page numbers where they are cited or supplement the text. I've also provided urls to online versions where available.

1
Reading Reduces Stress

> *"Losing yourself in a book is the ultimate relaxation."*
>
> — Dr. David Lewis

Reducing stress sounds like a huge benefit from reading, right?

Yes, but . . . let's start by recalling that stress has both positive and negative effects on us.

A double-edged sword

On the up side, stress experienced in the right moments and processed in the right ways can help us thrive in a variety of ways. In his book *Before Happiness*, Shawn

Achor cites studies showing that some stress can improve memory and cognitive performance, narrow our attention and increase brain processing speed, and enhance our resilience and immune systems. All these effects increase both our physical and psychological thriving.

Even severely traumatic experiences can deliver positive results: greater mental toughness, better social relationships, revised priorities, and sense of meaning. Researchers have dubbed this "post-traumatic growth" and they've identified ways of responding that can make growth more likely following these extreme stresses.

> *Some stress can ... improve both our physical and psychological thriving.*

Peterson, et al., described these growth attributes as:
- improved relationships with others
- openness to new possibilities
- greater appreciation of life
- enhanced personal strength
- spiritual development

On the down side, Achor acknowledges the important and "equally true" science showing that stress, particularly chronic, long-term stress, has been linked to a host of serious physical and mental health problems.

1. Reading Reduces Stress

To investigate what might influence such contrasting effects from stress, Achor constructed a simple experiment. Dividing workers in a high stress job environment, he showed one group a video warning of the debilitating effects of stress on health and work. The second group saw a video presenting several of the positive impacts of stress discussed above (e.g., increased mental focus and longer-term resilience).

The results were stark. The negative video group showed the expected ill effects of their stressful work environment. But simply making the other group *aware* that stress could have positive effects on them reduced their level of negative responses by 23%. And their productivity improved by nearly 30%.

Achor's advice: learn to recognize when you're feeling stress and identify the reason behind it, then refocus on how the stress might help you. You might be stressed about a work deadline or interviewing for a new job. But the reason behind the stress could be caring for your family, or your desire to move to a new city, or changing the life of your client.

Those are not random examples. At the same time I started work on this book in 2018, my wife Yvonne and I were dealing with major stress caused by our planned move back across the country to be closer to our families. I'm fortunate; having Yvonne at my side and knowing about the stress-management research discussed here kept the move from being totally overwhelming.

Armed with Achor's advice and aware of how stress can be a positive, we could harness the short-term stress to stay focused on the multitude of details. We could apply our brains' increased processing speed to stay calm and adjust on the fly to inevitable glitches, especially in the last days of packing and the four day drive from Colorado to upstate New York. And we could take comfort that neuro-science agrees, as long as it didn't kill us, the stress could make us stonger!

Plus, we both read daily, tapping into a key tool for reducing harmful stress. Now let's look at how that works.

Reducing negative stress helps more than our careers

A 2013 report from Canada's National Reading Campaign summarized research from Sussex University on how reading reduces stress as follows:

"Reading was proved:
- 68% better at reducing stress levels than listening to music;

1. Reading Reduces Stress

- 100% more effective than drinking a cup of tea;
- 300% better than going for a walk and
- 700% more than playing video games.

"Reading for as little as 6 minutes is sufficient to reduce stress levels by 60%, slowing heart beat, easing muscle tension and altering the state of mind."

Now, I certainly do agree that reducing – or at least better managing – stress at work can help us perform our jobs better.

But what about other areas of our lives?

The most ominous effects of too much stress are not poor performance on the job. To get more specific about the down side dangers, in *Healthy Brain, Happy Life*, Wendy Suzuki catalogs an alarming list of physical and mental disorders that chronic stress can lead to:

- heart disease
- depression
- cancer
- ulcers
- reproductive issues
- damage to specific areas of your brain (hippocampus, prefrontal cortex, and amygdala)

*Reading for **as little as 6 minutes** is sufficient to reduce stress levels by 60%*

While major illnesses related to stress can certainly diminish our performance at work, our overall health impacts every aspect of our lives.

More immediate, day-to-day effects of stress – irritability, distractedness, moodiness – likewise impact our personal relationships and outside activities as much as our work.

Reaping the stress-reducing rewards of reading

Dr. Suzuki offers several types of Brain Hacks (four minute exercises and activities) for overcoming stress. She designed hers to "interrupt [stress's] effects on our brains and bodies to lessen its impact." Her suggestions for interrupting stress include dancing to your favorite song, or savoring a cup of tea or coffee.

But then, those two extra minutes for reading produced 68% more stress reduction than music and 100% more than savoring a cup of tea!

And according to Dr. David Lewis, a similar interruption of stress occurs in our brains when we read. He explains:

> "Psychologists believe this is because the human mind has to concentrate on reading and the distraction of being

taken into a literary world eases the tensions in muscles and the heart."

True, the relaxing effect of reading was measured as taking six minutes, rather than the four that Dr. Suzuki's recommendations promise. But then, those two extra minutes of reading produced 68% more stress reduction than listening to music and 100% more than savoring a cup of tea!

Fact or fiction?

The Lewis quote describes one effect of reading as "being taken into a literary world." When Yvonne reached that phrase in her editor role, she raised a question about the value of reading non-fiction, business or self-development books, as opposed to the fictional stories (whether or not they ascend to the level of "literature").

As you'll see in several later chapters, whenever "either/or" questions arise, my answer is often, "Yes." Or, both. In this case, I have a couple of reasons.

First, we'll be exploring several benefits of reading for which I think the key driver is learning. I hope most will agree that we learn useful skills, like empathy, from fiction. But it seems fair to say that for learning, the scale tips more in favor of non-fiction.

We'll cover several ways that reading both supports and directly delivers "learning" in later chapters, too. But recall the Joan Westenberg quotation at the beginning of the Introduction, "My secret weapon is that I read."

Now add this one from Rick Hanson,

> "Learning is the superpower of superpowers, the one that grows the rest of them. If you want to steepen your growth curve in life, ***it pays to learn how to learn.***"

Keep that last phrase in mind as we journey through the benefits of reading and connect the dots on what our brains are up to when we read.

My second reason for saying read both, however, may bring the scale back to balance. Because the best non-fiction work often relies on stories. The best writers of non-fiction employ both true accounts of real-life examples and fictional tales used as analogies, metaphors, thought experiments, and the like.

True story: When I was in law school, I frequently had a good friend read over a draft of a class paper or legal article I was writing. He knew I wanted honest criticism and suggestions for improvement.

But he also knew that I would take one particular favorite phrase of his as the highest compliment he could give for feedback:

"Reads like a novel!"

Relax, as you read on.

2

Helps You Sleep

> *"There's something really intoxicating about getting lost in someone else's world for an hour or two before you get lost in your own dreams."*
>
> — Jayne Helfrick

Some of my favorite childhood memories involve bedtime stories being read to me and later reading myself to sleep. I continued the tradition with my own kids, to the point of reading both *The Hobbit* and the entire *Lord of the Rings* trilogy to them, aloud. I know, I'm weird.

But somewhere in adulthood I kicked the bedtime part of my reading addiction and followed the rest of our culture into closing out the evening with a lit screen, usually the television, in front of my face.

Then my business book meetup group chose *The Power of When*, by Michael Breus, in which he develops his theory of "chronotypes" and the best times of day (and night) for different types to engage in common activities. No surprise, sleep rhythms play a big role in his advice.

So I've revived my end of the evening reading habit, focusing this new reading time on fiction, since most of my other reading involves books, blogs, and other work-related information sources.

I confess the TV is usually still on until after Colbert's monologue. For some reason, that whole blue light problem has never seemed to keep me awake. If you suffer from insomnia, or even just take longer than you'd like to fall asleep, but don't want to turn off your devices, Breus's website has some technological solutions to the blue wavelength issue.

For me the renewed joy of reading fiction adds a bonus to the benefits from sleeping well.

What are those other benefits?

2. Helps You Sleep

More than physical restoration

I don't know about you, but I'd always viewed sleep as a restorative activity that helps us recover from physical work, injuries, and illnesses. Those are important, of course. But more recently I've learned that equally important brain activity goes on when we're sleeping.

Critical to my work, in 2014 Yang, et al., summarized earlier research showing the effects of sleep on learning this way:

> "Sleep has an important role in learning and memory consolidation. During sleep, neurons involved in wakeful experiences are reactivated in multiple brain regions, and neuronal networks exhibit various patterns of rhythmic activity."

Taking this research further, the study captured images showing the **same neurons** activated during motor learning exercise, were reactivated while in deep REM sleep.

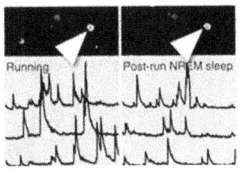
Same neuron firing during running and then sleeping

Another set of images showed that 24 hours after the motor learning, the neurons had formed new synapses.

In her book *Mindshift: Break Through Obstacles to Learning and Discover Your Hidden Potential*, Barbara Oakley highlights this finding and these fascinating images showing the newly grown neuron dendrite spines.

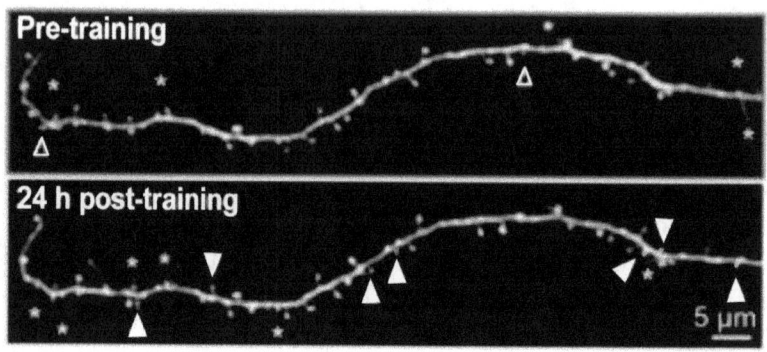

She calls learning something new, followed by sleep, "a magic combination."

To drive home the role of sleep, the researchers also looked at new spine formation after motor learning with normal sleep versus sleep deprivation. The sleepers had nearly twice as many newly formed dendrite spines.

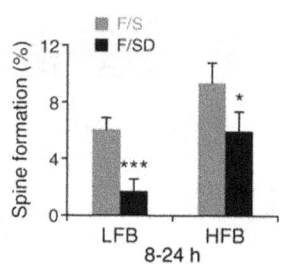

And the brain benefits we gain from proper sleep go beyond learning and memory. Sleeping has a critical role in helping our brains clear neurotoxins that accumulate while we're awake.

Sleep also drives creativity. It's been shown to facilitate those sudden bursts of insight we all have – you know, the ones we keep a notepad on the nightstand for – by helping our brains consolidate and restructure newly acquired information as we sleep.

In *Brain Rules: 12 Principles for Surviving and Thriving at Work, Home, and School,* John Medina described a prime benefit of sleep as avoiding the harms from going without it. He summarized research showing the impacts of sleep deprivation and formulated his rule on sleep this way:

> **Rule #7, Sleep Well, Think Well**
>
> . . . .
>
> "Loss of sleep hurts attention, executive function, working memory, mood, quantitative skills, logical reasoning, and even motor dexterity."

Sleeping well, of course, avoids all these brain function impairments.

What's reading got to do with sleep?

Back to Michael Breus and *The Power of When*. After reviewing some of the same scientific research showing the relaxation and cognitive benefits of reading we've just been covering, Breus echoes my own thoughts,

"Reading is a good addiction to have."

He notes the particular finding that reading lowers cortisol levels, "which will help you before bed" and concludes, "I recommend reading during your nightly Power-Down Hour in preparation for sleep."

The National Sleep Foundation website agrees, urging in its listing of Healthy Sleep Tips:

"Wind down. Your body needs time to shift into sleep mode, so spend the last hour before bed doing a calming activity such as reading."

Of course, reading only helps you sleep if you can put the book down. You'll still have to remember to turn out the light and get the amount of rest – including REM sleep – you'll need to process the information or experiences you're gaining.

> *"So spend the last hour before bed doing a calming activity such as reading."*

But reading just before sleep also puts those new learnings and experiences at the front of the line for your brain to work with while you sleep.

Read . . . **then** (i.e., at bedtime).

3

Improves Your Decision-Making Capacity

> *"[B]ecoming engrossed in a novel enhances connectivity in the brain and improves brain function."*
>
> — Christopher Bergland

I have to remind myself, as well as you, that we're talking about decision-making **capacity**, not magic!

We still have to apply our improved capacity to the problems at hand if we want to get better decisions. But with more capacity you'll have a better chance of making good choices.

So how does reading help increase your capacity?

Reading grows your brain

Until the last couple of decades, most scientists thought our brains were fully stocked at birth with all the brain cells we were ever going to get. Or maybe within the first few years of life.

But all that has changed. Now we have fMRIs and scanning technology that lets us see newly born neurons in adult mouse brains. We can even watch video of neurons forming new synapse connections – on YouTube!

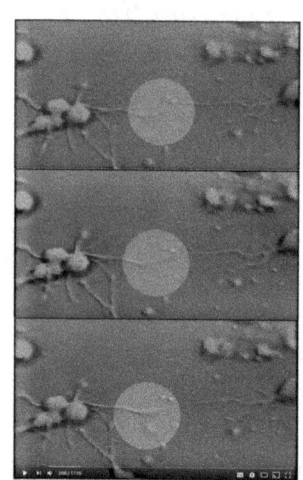

Quoting John Medina again, from *Brain Rules*:

"Researchers have shown that some regions of the adult brain stay as malleable as a baby's brain, so we can grow new connections, strengthen existing connections, and even create new neurons, allowing all of us to be lifelong learners."

Lots of research shows that as long as you keep breathing, your brain can keep growing. That in itself provides more capacity for decision-making.

Further research shows one of the best ways to stimulate the birth of new

3. Improves Your Decision-Making Capacity

neurons and incorporate them into the cognitive networks of your brain is by learning new skills. My favorite series of studies confirming the "brain-building" value of learning involved adults studying the streets of London while preparing for their taxi cab licensing exam, published by Maquire, et al., from 2000 to 2011. This small excerpt from the map of central London in the 2011 study gives a taste of how daunting a learning task they faced. The process has been given the most wonderful name: "acquiring the Knowledge."

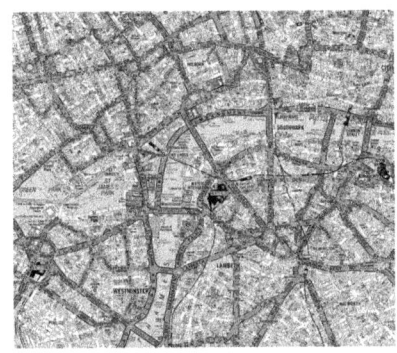

Acquiring "the Knowledge"

In the first study, cab drivers aged 32-62 years, who studied for an average of two years were compared to non-cab drivers. Researchers scanned their brains and focused on the structure associated with spatial learning and memory, the hippocampus. The cab drivers showed "significantly larger" posterior hippocampal volume than the non-cab drivers.

And between individual cab drivers, hippocampal volume correlated with the length of time they'd been driving. The longer they drove, the more they learned, the more hippocampal cells they grew.

Follow-up studies sought to eliminate possible reasons for the difference in volume other than studying and passing the exam. To account for the possibility that those who pass the cab licensing exam had innately better spatial ability and larger posterior hippocampi to begin with, researchers examined non-cab drivers with a wide range of navigational expertise. They found no association between expertise and volume in any parts of their brains.

Another study compared cab drivers to bus drivers with fixed routes to see whether driving-related factors like stress, as opposed to the cab drivers' challenges of applying their knowledge to constantly varying destinations, might be the cause of the hippocampal volume differences. The cab drivers still showed greater volume.

Moreover, the factor of "years of navigation experience correlated with hippocampal gray matter volume **only in taxi drivers**." The constant change and updating of their navigational experience seems to have greater brain volume impact than driving fixed routes.

Finally, researchers addressed the underlying question: Did "acquiring the Knowledge" itself lead to the increased

3. Improves Your Decision-Making Capacity

volume? In a longitudinal study, they gave a battery of cognitive tests and scanned the brains of a group of London cab driver trainees at the beginning of their training, along with a control group of non-cab drivers. They repeated these tests and scans 3-4 years later, after the trainees took their licensing exam, enabling comparison of results for those who passed, failed, and the control group.

The trainees who passed the exam showed both increased "volume in their posterior hippocampi and concomitant changes to their memory profile." Neither those who failed the exam, nor the control group showed structural changes in their brain scans. Wendy Suzuki reacted to these findings this way:

> *Learning (acquiring the Knowledge)* **caused** *adult brain volume growth.*
>
> *"Brain plasticity in the flesh."*

"Ta-da! Brain plasticity in the flesh!"

The researchers themselves concluded that acquiring the Knowledge, or in their words "engaging higher cognitive functions such as spatial memory" caused the repeatedly observed growth in the London cab drivers' brains.

Two side notes on growing your brain through learning

First, one contrary study made headlines in 2018, claiming that little or no neurogenesis occurs in human adult brains. In my opinion, that study suffers from small sample size, using dead or diseased tissue, and failing to offer any explanation for why so many others have found evidence for the opposite theory.

> "Neurogenesis is a process, not an event."

As other scientists from the pro adult neurogenesis camp put it, "they may just not have looked carefully enough" and,

> "Neurogenesis is a process, not an event. They just took dead tissue and looked at it at that moment in time."

Second, the London cab driver sequence of studies provided a cautionary lesson when the researchers checked on retired cab drivers. They found those who had stopped applying "the Knowledge" in their daily activity lost the brain matter volume advantage they had gained during their careers. Thus, while the studies showed brain growth at least into their sixties, the results also suggest it takes continued learning activity.

Use it, or lose it, right?

3. Improves Your Decision-Making Capacity

Reading, of course, is a primary method for learning. We're covering a variety of findings how reading helps us learn. But on this specific topic of growing your brain, another study specifically found,

> "the volume of white matter in an area of the brain that governs the use of language was increased following a six month daily **reading** program."

Fiction increases perspective, comprehension, and readiness to take action

Aside from growing and keeping a bigger brain, a 2013 study of neural "connectivity" before, during, and after reading a novel showed two specific effects of reading fiction that will help your decision-making.

First, scans showed after reading fiction there were increased neural network connections between areas of the brain associated with "perspective taking and story comprehension." Increasing your ability to perceive situations or understand concepts from multiple and alternative points of view certainly improves your chances of making wiser decisions. Improving your ability to comprehend story lines will help when you're examining possible outcomes from your decisions.

Second, the researchers found a longer term increase in connectivity in a brain region linked to "embodied semantics" – where our brains tie meanings of words and symbols to sensorimotor processing.

Taking action (or choosing not to) is the whole point.

A later review paper noted these sensorimotor areas are known to impact on the processing of **concrete, action-related** words and ideas. Taking action (or choosing not to) is the whole point of decision-making, right?

Building your "reading brain circuit"

In her book *Reader, Come Home*, Maryanne Wolf takes us through the science of what happens in our brains when we read, particularly when we engage in "deep reading." She breaks down into milliseconds the ways we process sentences and stories, employing our brains' areas related to images, language, empathy, analogy, inference, and creative thought.

Echoing the "problem exploration" and "draft-revise" meaning making processes we've discussed, Wolf writes:

> "It is hardly coincidental that what we think of as the methods of science characterize many of the most

3. Improves Your Decision-Making Capacity

sophisticated cognitive processes we deploy during deep reading."

But how can deep reading build on all these brain functions to increase our capacity for making decisions in the real world? Wolf goes on:

"The consistent strengthening of the connections among our analogical, inferential, empathic, and background knowledge processes generalizes well beyond reading. When we learn to connect these processes over and over in our reading, it becomes easier to apply to our own lives . . . Not only is it the basis for the compassionate side of empathy, but it also contributes to strategic thinking."

She sums up this "reading brain circuit" and its effect on our critical analysis abilities this way:

"It synthesizes the text's content with our background knowledge, analogies, deductions, inductions, and inferences and then uses this synthesis to evaluate the author's underlying assumptions, interpretations, and conclusions."

Perhaps most exciting, Wolf connects studies of brain imaging during creative thinking to the similar scans of brains engaged in "the last milliseconds" of deep reading, understanding, and insight "when we individual readers generate a single, new thought . . . ."

She poetically describes what readers find in those moments:

". . . the inestimable thoughts that from time to time irradiate our consciousness with brief, luminous glimpses of what lies outside the boundaries of all we thought before. In such moments, deep reading provides our finest vehicle to travel outside the circumferences of our lives."

And each time we exercise those critical analysis circuits in deep reading, each time we generate a new thought in those last milliseconds, we strengthen our neural "muscles" for facing up to our next tough choice.

> "[D]eep reading provides our finest vehicle to travel outside the circumferences of our lives."

Read on.

4
Makes You a Better Leader

*"A reader lives a thousand lives . . .
The man who never reads lives only one."*

— George R.R. Martin

The benefits of reading we've already covered go a long way toward making us better leaders. But one more that's been revealed by recent research might seem counter-intuitive: Reading helps you develop greater empathy.

A 2015 report from the UK found that readers scored higher than non-readers on multiple measures of:

- Understanding other people's feelings (65% vs. 48%)
- Awareness of other cultures (60% vs. 38%)

- Ease (47% vs. 38%) and enjoyment (38% vs. 25%) of conversing with strangers

Maryanne Wolf cites a host of recent neuroscience research to back up her core thesis on empathy:

> "The act of taking on the perspective and feelings of others is one of the most profound . . . contributions of the deep-reading process."

She highlights one study titled, "*Your Brain on Jane Austen*," showing that closely reading fiction activates brain regions involved with **both** what the characters are feeling **and** what they are doing. This finding that reading fiction also activates brain regions for movement and touch related to what the characters are doing, reminded me of a principle in *Leading with the Heart*, by Duke basketball coach Mike Krzyzewski:

> "*You do, you understand.*"

> "When teaching, always remember this simple phrase: 'You hear, you forget. You see, you remember. You do, you understand.'"

Coupled with the brain scan results showing when we're reading, our brains **simulate doing**, it's easier to see how deep reading promotes understanding.

Another paper showed that reading fiction involves "cognitive processes known to underlie both empathy and theory of mind."

From these and other studies, Wolf explains how fully deep reading, especially fiction, contributes to our development of greater empathy:

> "[W]hen we read fiction, the brain actively simulates the consciousness of another person, including those whom we would never otherwise even imagine knowing. . . . The reading circuitry is elaborated by such simulations; so also our daily lives, and so also the lives of those who would lead others."

Empathy as a core leadership skill

I noted above that the relationship of empathy to leadership skills may seem counter-intuitive to some. Too often we see interpersonal skills and character traits like empathy dismissed as "soft skills." Too often these are treated as less important for leadership than, say, past positions of authority or subject matter expertise.

For those who may have embraced that line of thinking, perhaps the U.S. Army

Field Manual on Leader Development might alter your approach. The manual lists empathy as a core character attribute for leaders.

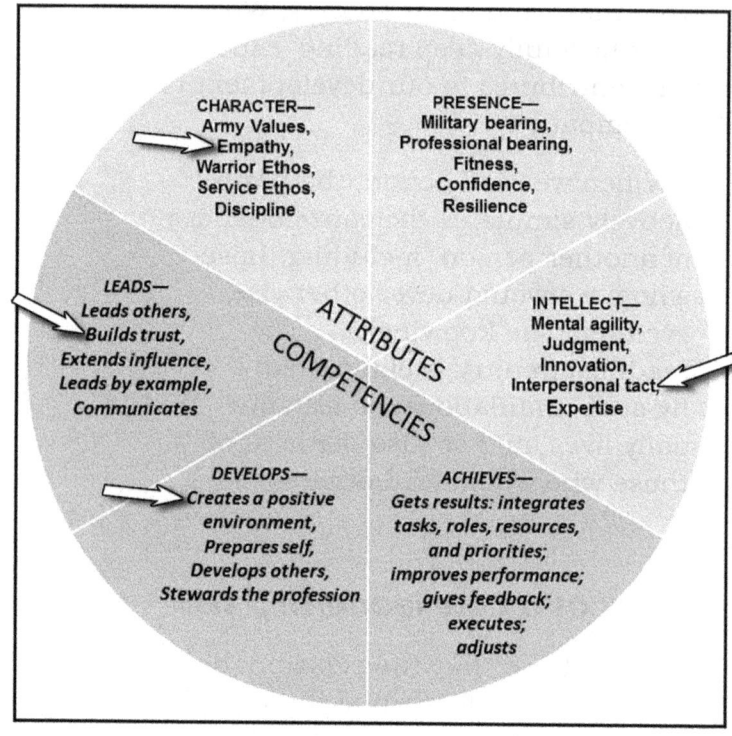

Army leadership requirements model

Addressing why empathy makes better leaders in a military setting, the manual explains:

> ". . . Empathy can help leaders to understand those that they deal with including other Soldiers, Army Civilians, local populace, and even

4. Makes You A Better Leader

enemy forces. Being able to see from another's viewpoint enables a leader to understand those around them better."

Consider this language on the military training importance of seeing "another's viewpoint" – including one's own soldiers, civilians, local populace, and enemy forces. Ask yourself how many times in the unknown future of your organization it might be valuable, even crucial, for its leaders to understand the viewpoint of a group of employees, a new customer segment, or local government officials (think Amazon's NYC headquarters saga)?

Then recall Wolf's analysis of brain scans while reading fiction. Her conclusion bears repeating: "when we read fiction, the brain actively simulates the consciousness of another person, including those whom we would never otherwise even imagine knowing."

Getting to the "doing" part, here's what the manual prescribes as performance indicators for leaders to display empathy as a strength:

> "Attentive to other's views and concerns. Takes personal action to improve the situation of Soldiers, Army, Civilians, family members, local community, and even that of potential adversaries. Breaks into

49

training, coaching, or counseling mode when needed and **role models empathy** for others."

In the workplace, empathy has been called the #1 leadership skill for business success. A recent report on leadership training announced,

> "Leaders who master listening and responding with empathy will **perform more than 40 percent higher** . . ."

Yes, this emphasis on empathy as a core leadership skill marks a dramatic change from the recent past. In his book *Emotional Intelligence*, Daniel Goleman noted a description of the 20th century corporate hierarchy as dominated by "the manipulative, jungle-fighter boss." He suggested that this model was undergoing a radical transformation toward one in which "the virtuoso in interpersonal skills is the corporate future."

At the outset of the book, Goleman identified empathy as **"the fundamental 'people skill.'"**

Many have observed as a truism that leadership can only exist in a relationship or interaction between the leader and those being led. Leadership scholar Warren Bennis compares this interaction with those

> "Effective leaders do so through . . . the practice of empathy."

4. Makes You A Better Leader

of conductor and orchestra, or coach and team. The leader must capture attention and communicate a shared vision.

> "As a leader, how do you capture the imagination of others? How do you communicate a vision?
> ... Effective leaders do so through the mastery of communication and ***the practice of empathy.***"

Bringing the necessity of empathy for effective leadership back to the military learning environment, consider Colin Powell's single sheet titled "The Powell Way" and listing ten skills and attributes of a good leader, culminating in "Empathy."

Of the failure to practice empathy in the broader business culture, Powell says,

> "Corporate leaders ought to learn that. Too often those at high levels don't quite understand the sacrifices and hardships of those at the bottom."

Indeed, all leaders ought to learn that. As the research summarized earlier shows, reading helps us develop more empathy by activating the brain regions involved in both the feelings and actions of characters. When we are reading, our brain "actively simulates the consciousness of another person" – a good working definition of practicing empathy.

Read, that's an order!

The Army manual also picks up where we started, specifying one of the ways for aspiring leaders to learn and develop greater empathy as a leadership skill:

> "**Read** relevant literature on empathy and social perspective taking."

Read on, soldier!

5

Makes You Smarter

> *"The smartest people I know read obsessively."*
>
> — Ageist.com editorial

If you're like me, you might be a little bit puzzled by this one. After all, what does getting "smarter" even mean?

I wondered, does smarter mean filling our brain with more information – trivia, some might call it – thus relating to its storage capacity? Or, does it refer to our brain's ability to process the information faster, make more connections between items, or increased recall from memory?

Well, when we're looking at the impact of reading on our brains, the answer is simply, yes.

The more you read, the more you know

I guess it should be obvious, but reading adds to your stockpile of information. Less obvious, perhaps, reading books and other long-form written material does it better than spoken words or tweets, for example.

In a 2001 report aptly entitled *What Reading Does for the Mind*, the authors point to several reasons that "reading yields significant dividends for everyone – not just for the 'smart kids' or the more able readers."

For example, they analyzed vocabulary richness of different sources and formats of text and other verbal information, from scientific abstracts, to adult books, to television, to everyday speech. Not surprisingly, books were shown to deliver three times greater word variety exposure than speech. They found books help build a richer vocabulary for engaging with and understanding the world around us.

Books deliver three times greater word variety than speech.

5. Makes You Smarter

More directly to the point, the authors reviewed a range of prior studies testing the relationship of "reading volume and declarative knowledge." Results showed that avid readers just plain know more about lots of disparate topics.

Their studies covered a wide range of general knowledge, and thus were intended to cover topics "relevant to daily living in a technological society in the late twentieth century." Questions chosen for the study asked about,

> *Avid readers just plain know more about lots of disparate topics.*

- what the carburetor in a car does (this study was conducted before most cars were switched to fuel injectors)
- the meaning of carcinogenic
- the effect on consumer loans when the Federal Reserve raises the prime interest rate

Reading volume accounted for 37.1% of the variance in overall content knowledge, even after accounting for other contributing factors like general ability, SAT scores, and exposure to other media.

Thus, reading helps you, me, everyone, accumulate more raw material for our brains to work with.

Reading improves your brain's processing power, too

What can you do with all that stored up knowledge? Or, more relevant to our discussion, what does reading help your brain do with it?

Again, a short answer: Lots.

So much, in fact, that we can only cover a few summaries of the relevant science in recent years. For example, a 2015 research review article analyzed years of results from studies on adult brain growth.

These studies show how brains respond to "enriched environments" (i.e., ones that both enable and require ongoing learning): they produce a mind numbing alphabet soup of brain chemicals, growth factors, proteins, and neurotransmitters. The review paper focused on the production and role of these chemicals in aging and adult neurogenesis.

Neuroscience calls the connection between actions we take and what happens to our brains at the cellular level "activity-dependent regulation." Two such activities have been shown especially helpful to brain function: physical exercise and living in a cognitively challenging environment.

5. Makes You Smarter

It's worth noting that most forms of exercise likely involve learning, too. We may be learning things directly related to the physical activity, the rules of a sport, a new route for our run, or more about our abilities and limitations. Or, we may be learning unrelated things while we work out, by listening to a podcast or just thinking about how the new information in a book we're reading fits into our prior knowledge.

But studies comparing the two suggest that the enriched environments (which include voluntary exercise opportunity) give even better results than exercise alone. Combined, they enhance cognitive function, increase brain growth chemicals, and help generate new neurons.

Bottom line, the more you put your brain and body to work learning new things, the more your brain grows and adapts to further enhance your capacity. It seems apparent that reading – the sort of deep reading Maryanne Wolf describes – puts your brain into a "cognitively challenging environment" as quickly and thoroughly as anything else you can do.

> *Deep reading puts your brain into a cognitively challenging environment as quickly and thoroughly as anything you can do.*

In *Brain Rules*, John Medina examined other research showing that "when people learn something, the wiring in their brains changes" and "acquiring even simple pieces of information involves the physical alteration of the structure of the neurons participating in the process."

He concludes:

> "The brain acts like a muscle: The more activity you do, the larger and more complex it can become."

Impressive evidence on the impact of learning emerged from the Synapse Project, Park, et al., in 2014. Studying the effects of different activities on aging brains, they showed that "sustained engagement in **cognitively demanding, novel activities**" yielded cognitive improvements in tests of

- mental control,
- visuospatial processing,
- and most dramatically, episodic memory.

The greatest of these brain benefits were shown in the groups that engaged in formal training to learn quilting or digital photography and photo editing skills, or both.

The study paper doesn't tell us whether the "formal training" involved reading. But I suspect it did. For two semesters in college, I was majoring in photography.

That was in the early 1970s, long before digital, of course. We spent a good deal of time reading from books about lighting, lenses, depth of field, composition, color theory, and the history of the art.

> *"The brain acts like a muscle: The more activity you do, the larger and more complex it can become."*

Another line of research focusing back on fiction showed that reading short stories helps us overcome what the researchers call a "need for cognitive closure" – our discomfort with ambiguity. The study notes other research finding that such discomfort can interfere with information processing, "leading to decreased creativity and rationality."

Researchers had groups of students read either essays or short stories matched for length, reading difficulty, and interests. Compared to the essay readers, the study found that the short story readers "experienced a significant decrease in self-reported need for cognitive closure" – i.e., they became more comfortable with ambiguity.

The researchers concluded with the suggestion that:

> "[R]eading fictional literature could lead to better procedures of processing information generally, including those of creativity."

Before leaving this study, however, one other reported result should be noted. This ambiguity-calming effect on the fiction readers was found to be "particularly strong for participants who were habitual readers (of either fiction or non-fiction)." My takeaway from this: reading **both** fiction and non-fiction helps us accumulate more raw material **and** more mental strength and agility.

When considering how reading helps us put our increased knowledge stockpile to use, recall the brain benefits that we've explored already, particularly in the decision-making and leadership chapters:

- more neurons,
- more connections,
- more white matter,
- greater empathy.

All these overlapping benefits work together, enhancing our brains' ability to process the information and experiences we gather from reading – all helping to make us "smarter."

Read on.

6
Helps You Live Longer

> *Do not read, as children do, to amuse yourself, or like the ambitious, for the purpose of instruction. No, read in order to live.*
>
> — Gustave Flaubert

Before we get to the science showing this extra benefit of reading, please take note of the two-pronged meaning in the phrase "helps you live longer." It really comes down to which word you put the emphasis on.

Live **longer**. And,

Live longer.

The distinction between these two meanings became more real for me after I "retired" – for the second time – a couple of years ago. Even when I speak that word aloud, it gets air quotes. I just don't have a "retiring" personality!

So it didn't surprise anyone who knows me that I was already talking about my next venture, Old Dog Learning. It began with my core coaching work, helping people who feel stuck transform their lives by learning what they need to find their next path.

As I studied methods and theories for getting unstuck and changing paths, a related theme emerged. I realized these feelings that we've become stuck and need to change paths often flow from the simple fact that we're living longer than past generations.

How much longer?

A 2009 study says, "most babies born since 2000 in [developed] countries . . . will celebrate their 100th birthdays." One of the authors has been quoted as saying, "a baby born today has a 40 per cent chance of **living for 150 years**."

And then there's Google's 2013 investment in Calico Labs, with a stated mission of "understanding the biology that controls lifespan" and "to devise interventions that enable people to lead

6. Helps You Live Longer

longer and healthier lives." According to a 2016 article from MIT Technology News, Calico's funding runs to $1.5 Billion.

The article quotes the former head of Google Ventures as saying **humans could live 500 years**. Quickly noting that's "unlikely" any time soon, the article explains Calico's well-funded scientists are "playing the long game."

The future is already here

Consider these U.S. age statistics:

- the 65+ age groups overall are fastest growing
- 85+ group expected to double by 2035 (to 11.8 million)
- 100+ group grew 43.6% (to 72,197) from 2000 to 2014

Now, ask yourself why do 74% of today's workers say they expect to continue working past 65?

A 3-stage life – learn, work, retire – no longer works.

Here's what those folks have realized: The 3-stage life – get an education, get a good job, and then "retire" to a life of leisure and comfort – no longer works. Not economically. Not emotionally.

63

I don't want to divert too far from our discussion of how reading helps you live longer, so I'll offer you a short reading list with titles that suggest both the economic and emotional aspects of the issue:

- *The 100-Year Life: Living and Working in an Age of Longevity,* by Lynda Gratton and Andrew Scott
- *The Longevity Economy: Unlocking the World's Fastest-Growing, Most Misunderstood Market,* by Joseph Coughlin
- *I've Decided to Live 120 Years: The Ancient Secret to Longevity, Vitality, and Life Transformation,* by Ilchi Lee
- *Wisdom@Work: The Making of a Modern Elder,* by Chip Conley

The issues go beyond the simple historical fact that we're living longer and staying healthy long past the traditional retirement age. These books uncover the parallel trend that has been cutting away the foundation of the 3-stage model: the pace of change in every aspect of life.

Technology ever more rapidly changes how we work, what we need to know to do those evolving jobs. New tools and ideas can start whole new industries (while eliminating others) in the span of a decade. The notion of getting a good job

6. Helps You Live Longer

to work at for 40-50 years has become quaint, if not delusional.

Similarly, the concept of a few "golden" years of retirement we were sold by Del Webb in the 1950s – days of little but golf, rocking chairs, and early-bird specials – no longer works. As demonstrated by the authors in *The 100-Year Life*, a combined pension and savings rate of around 9% of income for 40+ years of work, plus Social Security, would fund a retirement at 50% of your salary for (drum roll) **eight years**.

But now, the period of life after age 65 has grown to 20, 30, even 40+ years. (And will get longer still, if Calico has its way!) The same calculations for retirements of 20-35 years would require a savings rate of 17-25%. For 44 working years.

> *We'll need to get away from viewing life stages as some predetermined, linear sequence.*

The authors conclude that most people outside the top 1% will need to work into their 80s before they can afford this idealized retirement.

For me, that lifestyle has always seemed an intellectual and emotional wasteland, stripped of meaningful activity. But now, when viewed as a way to spend all our years **after** some arbitrary "retirement age," it has become unattainable for all but the wealthiest.

The books listed above, along with research papers, government reports, my work with clients and colleagues, led me to reflect on my own experience with a multi-stage life. They exposed, for me, an urgent need to redefine how we look at the stages of our lives. The researchers do suggest some possibilities. Most boil down to approaching life as consisting of four or five, roughly 20-year stages, perhaps alternating periods of learning, working, retooling, rejuvenating.

We are only beginning to experiment with new mindsets and methods needed to navigate our longer lives. Most crucial, we'll need to get away from viewing life stages as some predetermined, linear sequence. For example, author, boutique hotel chain founder, and more recently "Modern Elder" at Airbnb, Chip Conley has proposed moving your retirement from the last part of life to the middle.

I think we'll evolve toward even more – and shorter than 20-year – cycles of learning, work, and rejuvenating, probably overlapping them. One way or another, we must develop new models for smoothly navigating major changes in our work or other life pursuits that we may choose, or have forced upon us.

In my own work, these insights inspired me to expand my focus beyond "getting unstuck" to serving as a guide on clients' questing to add more meaning and joy to life, as so many of us keep living longer.

Now, back to . . .

How reading helps you **live longer**

Recall the Calico Labs mission: enabling longer and healthier lives. It's not just that our lives are getting longer in years. We're already staying healthy, active, independent, and productive much longer.

As a 2013 study reported,

> "89% of those aged 51–54 and 56% of those aged 85+ report no health-based limitations in work or housework."

That's where shifting the emphasis toward **living** longer comes in. As many of us live decades past the traditional retirement age with "no health-based limitations," how does reading help with both?

> *"56% of those aged 85+ report no health-based limitations in work or housework."*

It was the 2016 study, *A Chapter a Day: association of book reading with longevity*, by Bavishi, et al., that prompted me to add this sixth benefit of reading books. The researchers summed it up this way:

> "[T]he benefits of reading books include a longer life in which to read them."

67

In their sample of 3635 participants followed over 12 years, book readers lived significantly longer (4 months longer, or a 20% reduction in mortality) compared to readers of newspapers and magazines and non-readers. These results held even after controlling for "age, sex, race, education, comorbidities, self-rated health, wealth, marital status, and depression."

The authors expressed some surprise in one of their findings: that "any level of book reading gave a significantly stronger survival advantage than reading periodicals." To examine the difference found between reading books vs. periodicals, the authors focused on the participants' cognitive levels before and after. Their "finding suggests that reading books provide a survival advantage [over periodicals] due to the immersive nature that helps maintain cognitive status."

They did not, however, identify the types of periodicals being read. While I've probably shown my own bias toward books, I'm not ready to dismiss the value of reading in other formats. I suspect longer, info-packed and idea-rich articles in *The Economist* or *Science Magazine* deliver a more book-like, immersive reading experience than *People* or *Sports Illustrated*.

We've covered many other benefits that flow from reading and impact more on the "living" side of the phrase living longer. But even in this study where the authors were focused on the "longer" aspect, they still captured how reading impacts both in their concluding sentence:

> "The robustness of our findings suggest that reading books may not only introduce some **interesting ideas and characters**, it may also give more years of reading."

We'll have to wait for further study to sort out causation more precisely. But I'm inclined to think it's that "immersive nature" of the reading, more than the page count or binding style, that delivers the improvements in cognition.

In addition to the simple joy of reading.

Reading as a life multiplier

When the researchers talk about adding months (or Calico, decades and more), they're still thinking in terms of time as we measure it with clocks and calendars. And they're using addition.

But there's another way to consider how reading increases the span of your life. We hinted at it in the discussion of empathy as a leadership skill in Chapter 4, with the opening George R.R. Martin quote. There we referred to the power of reading to help us understand others by "living" their experiences in the act of reading.

Here, I'm taking Martin's observation that "a reader lives a thousand lives" more literally. And adding a twist to help you be more mindful about the "lives" you choose to multiply in yours.

In *On the Shortness of Life*, Seneca wrote that by reading the works of past thinkers, readers "really live." He explained

> "it's not just their own lifetime that they watch over carefully, but they annex every age to their own; all the years that have gone before are added to their own."

He wrote of debating, conversing, and cultivating relationships with authors, many long dead, and warned:

> "From them you'll take whatever you wish; it will be no fault of theirs if you fail to take in the very fullest amount you have room for."

Seneca focused on reading the works of philosophers. But recall how our brains simulate the thoughts and actions of fictional characters, too. Indeed, the full impact of this "life multiplier" effect includes gaining vitality from both the characters and the authors behind them.

So, read on ... and "really live."

7
Print or Digital

> *"When I read a manuscript ... I print it out. ... That helps me really read the words, pay closer attention, fully engage the story being told, **be** with it as I read it."*
>
> — Kerry Temple,
> editor of *Notre Dame Magazine*

This chapter began as a short section in the last one. I started to expand on the longevity study that emphasized the "survival value of the immersive nature" of reading books, compared to other formats. But the section kept growing.

As the quote above shows, this debate also takes us back to research discussed in earlier chapters, such as the studies showing how deep reading builds empathy when "the brain actively simulates the consciousness of another person."

Some advantages of print

Other studies reinforce that reading in books, especially print books, delivers the greatest cognitive improvements. For example, a 2014 study compared reading a mystery on a Kindle to a paperback. The researchers found the Kindle readers were "significantly worse" at recalling the order events occurred in the story.

Touching several of the points we've covered, the same researchers compared iPad to paper reading, finding that "paper readers did score higher on measures having to do with empathy, transportation and immersion, and narrative coherence, than iPad readers."

> "Paper readers did score higher on measures having to do with empathy and transportation and immersion, and narrative coherence."

Their suggestions about why readers learn more from print books resonate with me:

> "The haptic and tactile feedback of a Kindle does not provide the same support for mental reconstruction of a story as a print pocket book does.
>
> ". . . [The differences for Kindle readers] might have something to do with the fact that the fixity of a

text on paper, and this very gradual unfolding of paper as you progress through a story is some kind of sensory offload, supporting the visual sense of progress when you're reading."

This "sense of progress" idea matches my own experience, particularly with nonfiction. When I've neglected to take notes on a particular point, I often find myself with a good sense of where to find it, physically. I seem to know roughly where the printed information or concept lies within the thickness of the book, on the right or left page, and in the top, middle, or bottom of the text.

When I get close to what I'm looking for, I may find myself seeking specific visual cues like subheadings, sidebars, or paragraph layout – or even a scribbled note I left in the margin (yes, I often horrify Yvonne by writing in my books).

One theory on learning provides further support for both the printed book vs. digital text argument and my personal experience. In his book *How We Learn*, Benedict Carey describes research showing the way we learn language and music, for example, goes beyond the simplistic Pavlovian stimulus-response-repetition process.

Instead, *perceptual learning* theorizes that we draw on prior learning to help us recognize, discriminate, and organize new symbols.

> "The skill . . . is the same one we use to learn a new alphabet, at any age, whether Chinese characters, chemistry shorthand, or music notation. . . . After [learning letters] we begin reading words and sentences . . . we forget how hard it was to learn all those letters in the first place, never mind linking them to their corresponding sounds and blending them together into words and ideas.

Carey's point on perceptual learning goes to how we build on the basics we've mastered to accelerate our learning.

> "That is, the brain . . . takes the differences it has detected between similar-looking notes or letters or figures, and uses those to help decipher new, previously unseen material."

Music to your eyes

With that as learning theory background, Carey offers an example of learning music that I think spills over into how we learn from reading printed books. But because Yvonne warned me that she never studied

7. Print or Digital

music and had a hard time relating to his example, I'll start with a quick reminder that written music notes are placed by the composer on a set of five lines and the spaces between, called a staff. Sheet music usually shows a double (or "grand") staff with fancy symbols at the left called clefs. The upper one is the treble clef; the lower one is the bass clef. A single invisible line between the two staffs carries the note called Middle C.

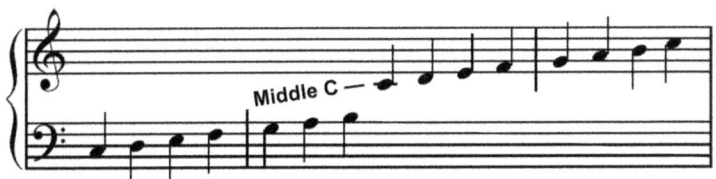

Each line and space on the staff tells us the pitch of a note placed there. As you go up from any line to the space above it, the note there goes up one level in pitch.

If it's been a long time (or forever) since your last music lesson, it may help to know that Middle C is the same as the beginning "Do" in the familiar music scale. So if you start at Middle C on the staff image above and go to the right, each note shown represents do, re, mi, fa, and so on.

Back to the example, now that we're all up to speed on the treble clef and middle-C. Here's Carey's explanation of how we use our visual knowledge of one note to learn new ones and the relationships between notes.

> "Once you've got middle-C nailed **on the treble clef**, you use it as a benchmark for nearby notes; when you nail the A an octave higher, you use that to read its neighbors; and so on."

I've emphasized "on the treble clef" because the clef allows us to place the notes in space and visually understand how each note relates to the others. If the note I see after "do" (middle-C) is placed two lines up, instead of the space immediately above, I learn quickly to jump from "do" to "sol," instead of "re."

As Carey put it,

> "To read even a simple melody, you have to be able to distinguish an A from a B-flat on the clef."

Something similar happens when we read from a printed book to learn new information, to reconstruct the melody of ideas placed by the author. The sequence letters, words, and sentences; the layout of paragraphs, lists, quotes, and callouts; the number of pages and the very thickness of chapters or sections; all provide a known physical structure with visual cues for processing the information, organizing it, and combining it with our prior knowledge.

Some downsides of digital

Digital formats tend to substitute fonts and flow the text to fit and fill whatever screen you're using at the moment. Or the text may scroll endlessly in one continuous page. And different devices or browsers may handle related non-text items (images, tables, and such) in a variety of ways. Indeed, for some purposes, these are strengths of digital.

But for learning new information, something is lost, too. Reading on screen seems to me a bit like attempting to learn new music by looking at notes without the staff.

Studies by lead author Ziming Liu may show us another side of the print or digital issue, indicating that skimming has become the normal way we read digital content. Based on eye-tracking studies, he descibes an "F" pattern in which readers quickly scan down the left side of the screen. They may glance at the conclusion and subheadings. Then, they attempt to "word-spot" and "cherry-pick" supporting details.

I use words like scan, glance, and attempt for digital reading, because the evidence of losses in comprehension and retention of details seem well established. Maryanne Wolf gathers more of this research in *Reader, Come Home.*

But she then describes her own experiment, using herself as the test subject, with perhaps more troubling results. She wanted to test whether her own digital reading – as a professor of reading and language research, she spends a lot of time looking at screens – had changed the way she read from print books.

She "gleefully" chose to reread Hesse's *The Glass Bead Game*, "one of the most influential books of [her] earlier years."

This time, she writes,

> "I could not read it. The style seemed obdurately opaque to me . . . The pace of action was impossible. . . . I hated the book.

She expressed her "scientific" findings about her reading abilities as follows:

> . . . [T]he inescapable conclusion was that . . . I now read on the surface and very quickly; in fact, I read too fast to comprehend deeper levels, which forced me to constantly go back and reread the same sentence over and over with increasing frustration; I was impatient with the number of clauses and phrases per sentence

. . . ; and finally, my so-called deep-reading processes never 'surfaced.'"

Remedial reading?

Unhappy with her results, Wolf tried yet again, modifying her experiment. This time she read in concentrated, 20-minute intervals, without a commitment to finish the book, or even how long she would stick to it. After two weeks, she had

> "returned to [her] former reading self. The pace of my reading now matched the pace of the action . . . I no longer imposed . . . either the speed or the spasmodic quality of attention that I had unconsciously grown accustomed to in my online reading style."

She sums up both the process that helped her recover her deep reading skill and some of the benefits we've been discussing:

> "In my case, only when I forced myself to enter the book did I experience, first, slowing down; second, becoming immersed in the other world in the book; and third, being lifted out of my own."

Digital reading is likely an inescapable part of our work and daily life. We're surrounded by glowing screens filled with ever-changing text. But Wolf's experiment gives us hope that we're not doomed by this to a reading life of hasty skimming, word-spotting, cherry-picking evidence, or a permanently "spasmodic quality of attention."

As we learned in Chapter 1 about stress, just being aware of an issue can help.

Wolf's self-study shows that, even when we spend lots of time reading digital formats, we retain the power to access our deep reading skills, to slow ourselves down and "enter the book." Fully reaping all the benefits of reading that we've covered likely depends on it.

Read on . . . and pace yourself . . . often in printed books!

8
Adopt Your Own Reading Plan

> *"The more that you read,*
> *the more things you will know.*
> *The more that you learn,*
> *the more places you'll go."*
>
> — Dr. Seuss

If you've read this far, I hope you've learned some new information about the benefits of reading. More importantly, I hope you're eagerly forming your own ideas about how to incorporate reading more effectively into your daily life.

While I'm revealing my hopes for this book, I hope you'll share what you've learned with friends and family. As my choice of the quote above hints, I hope our love of deep reading and printed books will continue across generations, starting them early – the younger, the better. If you're "young" like me, help your kids, grandkids, maybe even great-grandkids acquire a healthy reading habit.

> *"Each child – must build a wholly new reading circuit."*

Why the younger, the better? Maryanne Wolf makes a potentially scary point about the print vs. digital issue, rooted in the evolution of our species.

> "The act of learning to read added an entirely new circuit to our brains . . . learning to read deeply and well changed the very structure of that circuit's connections, which rewired the brain, which **transformed the nature of human thought**."

These deep reading circuits are not genetically wired into our brains. Not nearly enough time has passed for natural selection to achieve that. Humans reading long form text has been widespread only since the invention of the printing press, combined with the growth of institutionalized education in the last 200 years or so. Thus,

> "The reality is that each new reader – that is, each child – must build a wholly new reading circuit."

Her question for us about whether and how we will pass deep reading on to future

8. Adopting Your Own Reading Plan

generations and how our choices may impact their brains' capacities for "sophisticated intellectual processes" might seem chilling:

> "Will the time-consuming, cognitively demanding deep-reading processes atrophy or be gradually lost within a culture whose principal mediums advantage speed, immediacy, high levels of stimulation, multitasking, and large amounts of information?"

I don't pretend to know whether deep reading circuits and the cognitive skills they support provide long-term survival advantages over the sort of speedy, "spasmodic" attention Wolf herself found in her reading experiment. Nor whether digital reading may lead to rewiring our brains with circuits that support new capabilities right out of science fiction.

But for now, my bet is on both. (I know, where have you heard that before!) Given our earlier discussion of brain plasticity, I see no reason why we can't preserve our deep reading circuits while we build new ones to handle the digital reading tasks and habits that seem to be inherent in how we consume those media.

So, back to developing your reading plan. To prompt your thinking, you could read through the blog post, *Read More: 27 Ways To Get Reading This Year*. But on the chance that a list of 27 tips might seem more like tedium than treat, I've distilled three from that article, plus a bonus tip of my own.

3 Tips for adding more reading to your life

1. Read, routinely. Make reading a habit. If you're fortunate, reading will become an addiction for you. Feed it. Combining several of the methods from the *Read More* article:

- Set aside daily times for reading. Say, 10 minutes first thing in the morning and 10 more at bedtime. Block these times out and treat them as vital to your well-being. According to the article, this alone will allow you to read about 15 books per year!

> "Block these times out and treat them as vital to your well-being."

- Read all the time. Add to your "minimum daily requirement" by reading opportunistically. Use blocks of time you'd otherwise waste, like waiting in lines, sitting in reception rooms, parked outside your kids' school, and so on. Make reading your default down-time filler.

8. Adopting Your Own Reading Plan

- Keep your reading materials handy. Put books in your car, backpack, purse or jacket pocket. Keep several on your nightstand, one or more on side tables and counters in every room in your house and office. Add relevant magazines or printouts for reads you can finish in a few stray minutes.

I can attest to the combined value of these opportunistic reading habits. Yvonne almost always brings a book with her when we get into the car to go anywhere more than a few minutes away and spends most of the trip reading. If our errands include any stops where I'll need to wait for her, I bring one of the books I'm reading and take full advantage!

2. Read, freely. Or at whatever price fits your budget. Start with local libraries. Remember those? When we moved the last time, I didn't realize the value of having a public library in walking distance. After driving by it for months, I wandered in one day and got a card and I've been checking out an armload of books every few weeks ever since.

Plus, I gained access to an amazing range of online materials through the library website. If you're a student, you almost certainly have a wonderful physical library and online research and reading tools, as well. Of course, Google Books, Project Gutenberg, and others provide you with free access to public domain books.

More free or cheap sources: Bookmobiles, swap sites or groups, sharing with family and friends, used book stores, thrift shops with a book section, free ebooks, services like Kindle Unlimited and BookLender.com.

3. Read, deeply. And, read interactively. Many of the reading benefits we've learned about together flow from what cognitive scientists label deep reading – "slow, immersive, rich in sensory detail and emotional and moral complexity." If you're reading fiction, even moderately well-written, this kind of deep reading should happen automatically.

But for nonfiction, where you go for purposeful learning, deep reading may feel a bit more like work. It's well worth the effort, though, as our tour of the brain building and longevity benefits showed. And that's where reading interactively comes in, from two directions.

First, interact with the text. This might include following your place with your finger or bookmark. You might read aloud to yourself or to another. The most important tool when I'm trying to learn something new or master a difficult topic is: Take notes. I have three different ways I do this, depending generally on how I think I might use the material later.

If I'm reading in preparation for near term use, such as referring to a book in an upcoming presentation, I tend to place small Post-It notes on the edges of the pages next to the relevant text. Sometimes I write notes on the part of the Post-It that sticks out. When I bend the book's pages, the notes form a kind of quick index to the main points I want to share.

When I don't have a specific use I'm preparing for, I tend to underline and write notes in the margins, directly highlighting passages and ideas I want to remember. These notes might express my agreement, surprise, questioning of a point, or some connection to other work I've read. They will often form the seed of a future blog post, webinar, or talk. I designed the page layout of this book to provide you with wide margins on the outside – so please, experiment with your own ways of capturing your ideas in real time.

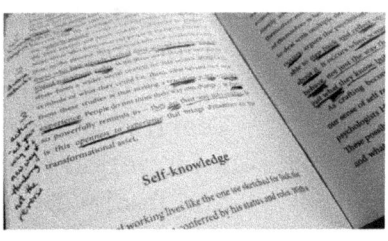

Sometimes I'm reading multiple books, articles, and online materials in an effort to learn a broader subject – in my work on helping people find their next path, for example. This kind of reading looks a lot like a multi-year course of study.

By now, I've read dozens of books on career shifting, happiness, aging well, creativity, neuro-science, learning – I even earned a U. Penn. specialization certificate comprising five courses in Positive Psychology. Most of my reading on these topics, I've annotated more expansively in notebooks. As you can see in the photo, when I get to this level of learning intensity, I'll often make notes in the margins of my notes!

Second, interact with others, about the text. Want a great way to make nonfiction reading more fun and less work? Tell others what you're learning. Teach it, gifting the valuable ideas or information casually to your friends and family, or presenting more formally in person or in your own writing.

One of the best ways I've found to do this in a fun setting, I joined a book club back in Boulder, CO. Named *Business, Books, and Brews*, the monthly reading and discussion focuses on self-development books. Do a quick search on MeetUp.com and you'll likely find a similar group in your area. If not, start one! (Look for my *Read 'Em & Reap* group, if you're in upstate NY.)

Bonus tip:
Subscribe, strategically

A couple of weeks after I started this project an email newsletter I subscribe to hit my inbox with that subject line you saw above and a link to the post, *Read More: 27 Ways To Get Reading This Year*.

Pretty lucky, eh?

Actually, this happens for me on a regular basis. So often, in fact, that in my early 2000s blog posts, I labeled it "discovery-by-serendipity."

The experience seems to flow naturally from subscribing to – and then actually reading – relevant blogs and newsletters. Relating then to my personal knowledge management (PKM) work, I began calling it "the planning-to-experience-serendipity side of PKM." In our business blogging boot camps and speaking at conferences, I took to describing this benefit of my reading addiction as "putting my lap where useful information can fall into it."

> *Put your lap where useful information can fall into it.*

89

It's easy to feel overwhelmed by the torrent of information spewing at us these days. It might seem that subscribing to have some of it intentionally aimed your way would only make it worse. But not if you're strategic about it.

> I recommend viewing your inbox and social media as a filter you can adust to remove more, or fewer, "contaminants" from your mental environment.

Instead of looking at your inbox as another firehose, I recommend viewing it as a valve that gives you control over the flow. Or a filter, where you can insert coarser or finer mesh to remove more or fewer "contaminants" from your mental environment. Or maybe like panning for gold, where you choose different gauge pans to control which information nuggets you'll capture.

Start with a strategy. Strategy starts with deciding what resources you want to pull in. It should not be hard to locate a half dozen or so thought leaders in whatever field you're working. That should be enough for their blogs or email newsletters to provide you with summaries, commentary on, and links to most of the latest issues, innovations, personalities, and trends affecting your work.

When I was starting out in legal knowledge management and information design work, I relied on a mix of generally relevant and precisely targeted blogs by law librarians and KM consultants to help me keep current and provide raw material for my own writing and commentary. You can still find some of the blogs I read then via the *Knowledge Aforethought* blogroll.

Keep it strategic. To keep your subscribing strategic, clean the filters now and then. As my work evolved (zig-zagged?) through book publishing, into consulting work in blogging and social media, I cancelled most of the law and KM subscriptions, added print book industry blogs and newsletters, then shifted again toward digital publishing and online marketing resources.

In addition to what you can discover in your email inbox, of course, social media continues to evolve as a potential filtering tool. For years, I found Twitter especially useful as an inbound information filter, by carefully following people for the same reasons I chose email subscriptions.

Using social media this way, however, requires paying more attention to choosing those you follow, while letting go of the usual focus on who – or should I say how many – are following you.

I confess that in recent years I had drifted toward counting my followers a bit, as my social media marketing role in BlogPaws grew. Now that I'm back working on my own, I suspect the pendulum may swing back.

I'm cautious, though. We've all seen the recent controversies over social media companies manipulating their algorithms to inhibit the free flow of information. Or worse, the sophisticated ways malicious individuals and organizations have filled these channels with false and misleading information should give us pause.

For now perhaps, strategic subscriptions pulled to your email inbox may remain the best method to experience your own discovery-by-seredipity.

Read on, for fun and profit!

9
Take Action

> *"Adults are much more likely to act their way into a new way of thinking than to think their way into a new way of acting."*
>
> — Richard Pascale

In his book *The Story of the Human Body*, evolutionary biologist Daniel Lieberman explains how extended periods of reading, doing it indoors, while sitting in comfy chairs may be contributing to increases in several of what he calls mismatch diseases. These include myopia (nearsightedness), obesity, and chronic low-back pain.

Before you freak out, he's not suggesting less reading! Far from it.

He opens his discussion of why we're finding increased myopia correlated with the spread of reading with this endorsement:

> "Reading is to the mind what exercise is to the body and is such an ordinary and essential activity . . . Sometimes when I am engrossed in a really good book, I lose conscious sense of my body and the world around me for hours at a time."

Lieberman reviews several hypotheses about why myopia has been a growing problem – especially in children – and how too much time spent indoors reading might be a contributing factor. In particular, he notes the evolutionary evidence that myopia has become much more prevalent since our inventions of writing and then the printing press.

Turning to the obesity and low-back pain epidemics, Lieberman points to "comfy chairs" and our overal attraction to the easy option: elevator over stairs, car over walking or biking, you get the idea. He even mentions reading **in** comfy chairs!

Again, he is not suggesting we abandon all forms of comfort and convenience, and certainly not that we stop reading. But he did mention in the myopia discussion that an obvious solution would be for children to spend more time outside. I immediately

9. Take Action

saw another image that I believe came from a Disney cartoon of Ichabod Crane walking down the road with his arm stretched out straight in front of him, reading a book.

To evade all the *Sleepy Hollow* storylines, I offer this image as a symbol for our movement – and I choose the word "movement" with purpose. Remember my tips to schedule realistically doable small blocks of reading time, but then add reading "all the time" and "everywhere"?

The idea is to find small chunks of time to read opportunistically. Try reading standing up, or even walking, when the opportunity arises and the location lends itself to doing so safely.

Recall as well, Maryanne Wolf's second experiment on herself, where she read in 20-minute chunks and recovered her deep reading skills. Like her, many of us spend much of our work time on screens of one sort or another. Try a standup or treadmill desk, for your screen work and for reading books, too. (I once claimed a section of our tall kitchen island counter as my office annex, with my laptop and a stack of books competing with the decor. Once again, annoying to Yvonne. I loved alternating standing and sitting, but I know there are better locations, eh?)

Lieberman closes out his story of the human body's evolution, past and ongoing, with a chapter called "Survival of the Fitter." This thread, reminding us that our brains and our ability to use them depend on our bodies, runs through several of the books on brain health I've mentioned. Indeed, John Medina's Brain Rule #1 is "Exercise boosts brain power."

And in a chapter subtitled "Exercise Can Make You Smarter," Wendy Suzuki offers a list of 4-minute workouts. Echoes from Chapter 5 above, where we noted that the brain acts like a muscle. Perhaps we should envision alternating 20-minute reading and 4-minute physical exercise sessions as a workout, the ultimate full brain-body fitness routine.

Alternating 20-minute reading and 4-minute physical exercise: the **ultimate brain-body fitness routine***!*

Which leads us to what I really mean by "Take Action." In discussing decision-making we noted,

> Taking action (or choosing not to) is the whole point of decision-making, right?

That notion applies to all the reading benefits we've discussed. Same for body fitness. What's the point of getting and keeping your brain and body all bulked-up and buff, full of knowledge and empathy, strength and energy, if you're not going to use them?

9. Take Action

Been reading non-fiction books to grow a new set of skill-related circuits in your brain? Practice them in your work! Start a new business on the side! Get moving!

If you're working in an organization, here's an example you might adapt. Back when I served on the training committee at my old law firm, we had a pass-it-on policy on attending continuing education conferences. The firm paid expenses for travel and registration. In return, lawyers had to share what they'd learned at a lunchtime presentation.

Your organization might apply this to reading, starting by emulating this employee benefit at tech company Buffer.com:

> "We give all teammates and their partners a new Kindle when they join and unlimited Kindle books whenever they'd like. This year, our reading perk expanded to include physical books as well as Audible subscriptions."

But don't let the reading benefits stop at the inside of each one's skull! Require them to share. A reciprocal reading benefit program might ask employees to:

- share book recommendations on the company email system
- write up book reviews for the company blog

- prepare and deliver a video or live presentation on a topic from several related books
- lead a team to develop and implement a new internal system described in books recently read
- create and launch a new customer product or service derived from all that learning

Developing programs for organizations, or habits for yourself, that put new learning into action becomes critically important when you feel hopelessly stuck trying to solve a problem. As Dr. Timothy Butler advised in *Getting Unstuck*:

> "We must find the will to act . . . The final step [to overcome] impasse is integrating what we've learned so we can make a decision **and take action**."

Review my suggestions for a "reciprocal reading benefits program" at work. Now consider which ones you should require of yourself, if your organization doesn't have such a program. Or, if you're working solo.

With fiction, taking action may more often involve some of those "soft" skills we've covered, like empathy and communication. For example, have you read a novel that gave you a new insight into an important relationship? Talk about it with that person in your life. Or go ahead and try out the interaction you've learned. Get moving!

9. Take Action

Don't stop at reading, learning, staying healthy. Put those capacities into action. Keep moving!

That's the true meaning of our "movement" symbol.

I'll close by urging a specific action for you to take that will put your reading to good use. It's a simple brain-body fitness regimen, using a piece of exercise equipment you almost certainly have at your fingertips: a pen or keyboard. Get those fingers moving, too!

Faulkner expressed it this way:

> "Read, read, read. Read everything – trash, classics, good and bad, and see how they do it. Just like a carpenter who works as an apprentice and studies the master. Read! You'll absorb it. **Then write.**"

The act of writing will help you consolidate, organize, and build on what you're learning in your reading. You don't need to publish or even write for anyone else's eyes. Private journaling and even random doodling can perform this dot-connecting function quite well. Which may help you take other forms of action.

But honestly, I hope you'll write to share the benefits of your reading. Toni Morrison is quoted as saying, "If there's a book that you want to read, but it hasn't yet been written, then you must write it."

I'm not disagreeing with her message, but in a practical sense, I can't write **all** the not-yet-written books I'd want to read. Or even know what those books should be about. So I want to read yours, too.

As I hope came through in the discussions of deep reading and print vs. digital – and in my confessions about my reading addiction – I don't mean you have to write a book, either. When you're ready to share what you're learning, you may prefer to start with a blog post, a short story, or a handwritten note.

What I'm getting at is captured in this sentiment from J.D. Salinger:

> "What really knocks me out is a book that, when you're all done reading it, you wish the author that wrote it was a terrific friend of yours and you could call him up on the phone whenever you felt like it."

Much as I love them, you can substitute any other form of well-written idea for the word "book" – an insightful blog post, a pithy Tweet, an artful poem, a thoughtful email. That's why I want to read yours.

Take action. Write . . . to yourself, to me, to the world.

Conclusion: As You Read

> "As you read these words, information flows from this book to you as patterns of energy shared between us."
>
> — Dr. Daniel J. Siegel

In the quote above, from *Mind: A Journey to the Heart of Being Human*, Siegel's description of the interpersonal neural processing that makes up our minds comes across as almost mystical. Recall from the Preface his proposal – grounded in recent science – that we view the human mind as an emergent complex system of energy and information flowing both within and between us. *MWe*.

I find it appealing, this notion of our minds connecting – and of reading books as a conduit for those connections.

So I'll leave you with a few more quotes about the lifelong (or is it, long life?) joys and benefits of reading, of writing, and of books.

But wait! I wrote the sentence above before some of my early readers posed their "challenging questions" that prompted me to add the Preface. My deep dive into deep reading revealed just how connected those joys and benefits of reading, writing, and books may be to our intellectual lives.

In *Deep Reading*, Patrick Sullivan proposes explicitly

> "that we theorize writing as a form of deep reading and learning – an . . . inquiry built around reading . . . essential for the development of mature meaning-making."

Does this theory bring you "troublesome knowledge" or pose challenging questions?

If you're inspired to read more and, perhaps, write more, then this book has become what I suggested books can be: a synapse for energy and information flow within and between us. In that metaphor, our writing could be viewed as pumping seratonin and dopamine into the synapse.

Or, using Louise Roseblatt's image of reading as "a combustion fed by the coming together" then, perhaps we should view writing as **pouring on accelerant!**

Conclusion: As You Read

May some of these closing thoughts ignite that spark and fuel that flame:

> "Books are the plane, and the train, and the road. They are the destination, and the journey. They are home."
> — Anna Quindlen

> "I cannot remember the books I've read any more than the meals I have eaten; even so, they have made me."
> — Ralph Waldo Emerson

> "Reading furnishes the mind only with materials of knowledge; it is thinking that makes what we read ours."
> — John Locke

> "No book is really worth reading at the age of ten which is not equally – and often far more – worth reading at the age of fifty and beyond."
> — C.S. Lewis

> "Books are humanity in print."
> — Barbara Tuchman

> "Think before you speak. Read before you think."
> — Fran Lebowitz

Again, I urge you to use the extra white space on these pages to add and explore your own ideas!

"Fairy tales are more than true: not because they tell us that dragons exist, but because they tell us that dragons can be beaten."
— Neil Gaiman

"Sometimes, you read a book and it fills you with this weird evangelical zeal, and you become convinced that the shattered world will never be put back together unless and until all living humans read the book."
— John Green

"If you don't have time to read, you don't have the time (or the tools) to write. Simple as that."
— Stephen King

"Start writing, no matter what. The water does not flow until the faucet is turned on."
— Louis L'Amour

"The best effect of any book is that it excites the reader to self activity."
— Thomas Carlyle

Conclusion: As You Read

"[W]hat sublimity of mind was his who dreamed of finding means to communicate his deepest thoughts to any other person, though distant by mighty intervals of place and time! Of talking with those who are in India; of speaking to those who are not yet born and will not be born for a thousand or ten thousand years; and with what facility, by the different arrangements of twenty characters upon a page!"
— Galileo

And finally, may

". . . these words reach from within me to between us to within you."
— Daniel Siegel

Now, don't just sit there reading.

TAKE ACTION!

Still here?

Okay, then I'll play the Marvel movie game and give you one more scene. This one contains a quote within a quote from an Inc.com article, with a title that I just love, *Why You Should Surround Yourself with More Books Than You'll Ever Have Time to Read.*

[Scene opens] Camera pans around Umberto Eco's personal library of some 30,000 volumes, then slowly zooms in on a heavy oak desk with open books stacked around a laptop. It's *you* sitting there and you're typing fast. You stop and glare intensely at one pile, before pulling out the third book down. You trace a finger over the page left open, finding the passage you need.

You look up as *Inc* writer Jessica Stillman enters, sits down, and reads aloud from her article:

> "Did Eco actually read all those books? Of course not, but that wasn't the point of surrounding himself with so much potential but as-yet-unrealized knowledge. By providing a constant reminder of all the things he didn't know, Eco's library kept him intellectually hungry and perpetually curious. . . . [Nassim] Taleb writes:
>
>> "A private library is not an ego-boosting appendage but a research tool. Read books are far less valuable than

unread ones. The library should contain as much of what you do not know as your financial means, mortgage rates, and the currently tight real-estate market allows you to put there. . . . Indeed, the more you know, the larger the rows of unread books. . . ."

["Your unread books are," Jessica paraphrases,] "a powerful reminder of your limitations — the vast quantity of things you don't know, half-know, or will one day realize you're wrong about. By living with that reminder daily you can nudge yourself toward the kind of intellectual humility that improves decision-making and drives learning."

You smile and nod, gaze around, then get up and walk over to a case filled with books, as yet unread by you, run a hand across a few bindings, a longing look on your face. Then you turn with purpose and head back to your work. **[Scene closes]**

It's worth noting that Stillman equates an "overflowing" e-reader with bulging print book shelves. And I'll add that audio books provide another way to "read" more.

I put **you** in this scene for a reason, you know. Yet again, I say, READ ON!

And TAKE ACTION!

Yes, BOTH!

Indexed References

On citation form: I've lived through being required to conform to APA, MLA, Chicago, and for the longest stretch, the Harvard Bluebook legal citation system. All I care about now are clarity and (reasonable) consistency. I don't believe you'll have any trouble identifying or locating any of my references as formatted.

I'm also going to post this index on the Old Dog Learning blogsite book page as a separate PDF with live links to every source that shows a url here.

Preface: on Deep Reading (and "MWe")

Page 1 –

"Deep reading … is a process …" – Patrick Sullivan, *"Deep Reading" as a Threshold Concept in Composition Studies*, in *Deep Reading: Teaching Reading in the Writing Classroom*, National Council of Teachers of English (2017), pg. 143, https://www.amazon.com/Deep-Reading-Teaching-Writing-Classroom/dp/0814110630/

"collaboration is at the heart of what MWe can do …" – *Mind: A Journey to the Heart of Being Human*, Daniel Siegel, M.D. (2017), pg. 326, https://www.amazon.com/Mind-Journey-Norton-Interpersonal-Neurobiology/dp/039371053X

Pages 2-3 –

"two main approaches to reading …" – educational theory background and Louise Roseblatt, Marcel Proust quotes from *Deep Reading: Teaching Reading in the Writing Classroom*, Introduction, pgs. xiii-xx, and Ch. 1, pgs. 6-20

Page 4 –

"a helpful book on teaching deep reading …" – *What Readers Really Do: Teaching the Process of Meaning Making*, Dorothy Barnhouse and Vicki Vinton (2012), pg. 51, https://www.amazon.com/What-Readers-Really-Do-Teaching/dp/0325030731/

Pages 5-6 –

"The term 'MWe' …" – *Mind: A Journey to the Heart of Being Human*, ibid, pgs. 37, 155-156, and passim

Pages 6-7 –

"inspires my call for intergenerational reading ..." – *Thirty Million Words: Building a Child's Brain*, Dana Suskind, M.D. (2015), pgs. 66, 72

"Siegel offers the pronoun MWe ..." – *Mind*, ibid., pg. 322

Page 8 –

"famous Stanford commencement address ..." – *'You've got to find what you love,' Jobs says*, https://news.stanford.edu/2005/06/14/jobs-061505/

"Bennis picked up on ..." – *Organizing Genius: The Secrets of Creative Collaboration*, Warren Bennis and Patricia Ward Biederman (1998), p. 66 https://www.amazon.com/Organizing-Genius-Secrets-Creative-Collaboration/dp/0201339897

Page 9 –

"my inaugural blog post back in 2003 ..." – *Knowledge Aforethought* blog, http://knowledgeaforethought.blogs.com/; in that first blog post, I wrote:

"Creative problem solving is often described as 'connecting the dots' and I like that image so much it's the basis for my company logo. But, as Warren Bennis pointed out in Organizing Genius, the best creative problem solvers have accumulated 'a vast number of experiential dots to connect.' "

http://knowledgeaforethought.blogs.com/knowledge_aforethought/2003/12/a_blog_for_lega.html

"I kept the Chilton DIY manual ..." – Chilton DIY Manuals, automotive repair manuals for specific make, model, year, https://www.chiltondiymanuals.com/repairmanuals

"running pool installation crews ..." – Fanta-Sea Pools, 36 page installation manual, https://www.poolsupplies.com/pdfs/fssolarpoolinstructions.pdf

Page 11 –

"connecting via the Old Dog Learning blogsite ..." – https://olddoglearning.com/author/tom-collins/

Pages 11-12 –

"Your "CUE" comes from ..." – *What Readers Really Do*, supra, pgs. 42-44

Introduction

Page 13 –

"**My secret weapon ...**" – Joan Westenberg, *Here's My Secret Weapon: I Read*, https://medium.com/hi-my-name-is-jon/heres-my-secret-weapon-i-read-a5d4b753efe4

"**still going strong since 2017 ...**" – DuckTales 2017, https://en.wikipedia.org/wiki/DuckTales_(2017_TV_series)

Page 14 –

Cartoon panel image – used only to illustrate text reference to Disney characters' relationships, personalities, and typical plot lines in Donald Duck comic books; Image Source: https://en.wikipedia.org/wiki/Huey,_Dewey,_and_Louie

Page 15 –

"**female journalism pioneer ...**" – see Wikipedia article on Margaret Fuller (1810-1850), https://en.wikipedia.org/wiki/Margaret_Fuller

"**a few recent titles: ...**" – *Why Leaders Must Be Readers*, Forbes (2012), https://www.forbes.com/sites/85broads/2012/08/03/why-leaders-must-be-readers/#1845b4bb4736; *For Those Who Want to Lead, Read*, Harvard Business Review (2012), https://hbr.org/2012/08/for-those-who-want-to-lead-rea; *5 Ways Reading Makes You a Better Leader*, Michael Hyatt blog (2015), https://michaelhyatt.com/science-readers-leaders/; *4 Reasons Good Leaders Are Readers*, Jeremy Kingsley blog (2017), http://jeremykingsley.com/4-reasons-good-leaders-are-readers/; *5 Science-Backed Reasons Why Readers Do Better in Their Careers*, Jesse Wisnewski on The Muse blog (2017), https://www.themuse.com/advice/5-sciencebacked-reasons-why-readers-do-better-in-their-careers

Page 16 –

"**The first five chapters will build and expand on ...**" – *5 Science-Backed Reasons Why Readers Do Better in Their Careers*, Jesse Wisnewski on The Muse blog (2017), https://www.themuse.com/advice/5-sciencebacked-reasons-why-readers-do-better-in-their-careers

Ch. 1 - Reading Reduces Stress

Page 19 –

"Losing yourself in a book ..." – quoting cognitive neuropsychology researcher David Lewis, in *Reading 'can help reduce stress'*, The Telegraph, Mar. 30, 2009, http://www.telegraph.co.uk/news/health/news/5070874/Reading-can-help-reduce-stress.html

"On the up side, ..." – *Before Happiness: The 5 Hidden Keys to Achieving Success, Spreading Happiness, and Sustaining Positive Change*, Shawn Achor (2013), pgs. 29-33 https://www.amazon.com/Before-Happiness-Achieving-Spreading-SustainingPositive-ebook/dp/B00BVJG2P6

Page 20 –

"can improve memory ..." – Larry Cahill, et al., *Enhanced Human Memory Consolidation With Post-Learning Stress: Interaction With the Degree of Arousal at Encoding* (2003), https://www.ncbi.nlm.nih.gov/pmc/articles/PMC202317/

"increase brain processing speed ..." – P.A. Hancock, et al., *On time distortion under stress* (2005), http://peterhancock.ucf.edu/wp-content/uploads/sites/175/2012/03/Hancock_Weaver_On-time-distortions-under-stress_2005.pdf

"enhance our resilience ..." – Elissa S. Epel, et al., *Embodying Psychological Thriving: Physical Thriving in Response to Stress* (1998), https://static1.squarespace.com/static/5769e57fd482e96c7680343c/t/58dabcdde58c6256ee677248/1490730207221/Epel+et+al.+1998.pdf

"and immune systems ..." – Firdaus Dhabhar, et al., *Study explains how stress can boost immune system* (2012), https://med.stanford.edu/news/all-news/2012/06/study-explains-how-stress-can-boost-immune-system.html; research paper, https://www.ncbi.nlm.nih.gov/pmc/articles/PMC3412918/

"dubbed this 'post-traumatic growth' ..." – Lorna Collier, *Growth after trauma: Why are some people more resilient than others—and can it be taught?* (2016), http://www.apa.org/monitor/2016/11/growth-trauma.aspx

"These growth attributes ..." – Christopher Peterson, et al., *Strengths of Character and Posttraumatic Growth* (2008), https://deepblue.lib.umich.edu/bitstream/handle/2027.42/58571/20332_ftp.pdf

"On the down side ..." – *Before Happiness*, ibid, pgs. 30-32

"serious physical and mental health problems ..." – George P. Chrousos, *Stress and disorders of the stress system* (2009), https://www.researchgate.net/profile/George_Chrousos/publication/26258826_Stress_and_disorders_of_the_stress_system/links/09e4150f0899bf1a02000000/Stress-and-disorders-of-the-stress-system.pdf

Page 22 –

"Canada's National Reading Campaign report ..." – National Reading Campaign, *Reading Facts* (2013), http://nationalreadingcampaign.ca/wp-content/uploads/2013/09/ReadingFacts1.pdf

Page 23 –

"The most ominous effects of too much stress ..." – *Healthy Brain, Happy Life: A Personal Program to Activate Your Brain and Do Everything Better*, Wendy Suzuki, PhD (2015), ch. 7, https://www.amazon.com/Healthy-Brain-Happy-Life-Everything/dp/0062366785/

Page 24 –

"Brain Hacks ... for overcoming stress ..." – ibid., pgs. 7, 184.

"And according to Dr. David Lewis ..." – *Reading 'can help reduce stress'*, The Telegraph, Mar. 30, 2009, http://www.telegraph.co.uk/news/health/news/5070874/Reading-can-help-reduce-stress.html

Page 26 –

"Learning is the superpower of superpowers ..." – *Resilient: How to Grow an Unshakable Core of Calm, Strength, and Happiness*, Rick Hanson (2018), pg. 50.

Ch. 2 - Helps You Sleep

Page 29 –

"something really intoxicating ..." – Jayne Helfrick, *How Reading Before Bedtime Can Help You Sleep, Dream And Be Better*, EliteDaily.com article, Apr. 23, 2015

Page 30 –

"theory of 'chronotypes' ..." – *The Power of When: Discover Your Chronotype--and the Best Time to Eat Lunch, Ask for a Raise, Have Sex, Write a Novel, Take Your Meds, and More*, Michael Breus (2016), https://www.amazon.com/Power-When-Discover-Chronotype-Lunch/dp/0316391263/

"**solutions to the blue wavelength issue ...**" – *The Power of When* website, Blue Light Product Recommendations downloadable PDF, http://thepowerofwhen.com/wp-content/uploads/2016/09/Blue-Light-Products-Breus.pdf

Page 31 –

"**effect of sleep on learning ...**" – Guang Yang, et al., *Sleep promotes branch-specific formation of dendritic spines after learning* (2014), https://www.ncbi.nlm.nih.gov/pmc/articles/PMC4447313/

"**the study captured images ...**" – Excerpted image from Yang, et al., *Sleep promotes branch-specific formation of dendritic spines after learning* (2014), Fig. 1, https://www.ncbi.nlm.nih.gov/pmc/articles/PMC4447313/figure/F1/

"**In her book *Mindshift* ...**" – *Mindshift: Break Through Obstacles to Learning and Discover Your Hidden Potential*, Barbara Oakley (2017), pg. 34, https://www.amazon.com/Mindshift-Obstacles-Learning-Discover-Potential/dp/1101982853/

Page 32 –

"**The sleepers had nearly twice as many ...**" – Yang, et al., image excerpted from Fig. 2, https://www.ncbi.nlm.nih.gov/pmc/articles/PMC4447313/figure/F2/

"**Sleeping has a critical role ...**" – Lulu Xie, et al., *Sleep Drives Metabolite Clearance from the Adult Brain*, https://www.ncbi.nlm.nih.gov/pmc/articles/PMC3880190/

Page 33 –

"**sudden bursts of insight we all have ...**" – Ullrich Wagner, et al., *Sleep inspires insight*, https://www.ncbi.nlm.nih.gov/pubmed/14737168

"**research showing the impacts of sleep loss ...**" – *Brain Rules: 12 Principles for Surviving and Thriving at Work, Home, and School*, John Medina (2008), pg. 168, https://www.amazon.com/Brain-Rules-Updated-Expanded-Principles/dp/098326337X/

Page 34 –

"**Reading is a good addiction ...**" – Michael Breus, *The Power of When* (2016), pgs. 307-309, https://www.amazon.com/Power-When-Discover-Chronotype-Lunch/dp/0316391263/

"**reading lowers cortisol levels ...**" – ibid., refers to the David Lewis research discussed in Ch. 1 on stress reduction

INDEXED REFERENCES

"calming activity such as reading ..." – National Sleep Foundation, *Healthy Sleep Tips*, https://sleepfoundation.org/sleep-tools-tips/healthy-sleep-tips/page/0/1

Ch. 3 - Improves Your Decision-Making Capacity

Page 35 –

"[B]ecoming engrossed in a novel ..." – Christopher Bergland, *Reading Fiction Improves Brain Connectivity and Function*, PsychologyToday.com article, https://www.psychologytoday.com/blog/the-athletes-way/201401/reading-fiction-improves-brain-connectivity-and-function

Page 36 –

"newly born neurons in adult mouse brains ..." – Henriette van Praag, et al., *Running increases cell proliferation and neurogenesis in the adult mouse dentate gyrus*, https://www.researchgate.net/publication/13103421_Running_increases_cell_proliferation_and_neurogenesis_in_the_adult_mouse_dentate_gyrus

"neurons forming new synapse connections ..." – Dr. Joe Dispenza - TEDx Talk, starting at 1:54 min., clip shows how neurons form new synapse connections during learning, including reading to learn new information, https://www.youtube.com/watch?v=7mW_vdaDrL8; image excerpted here shows three still frames from the clip shown by Dr. Dispenza during his talk

"malleable as a baby's brain ..." – *Brain Rules*, ibid, pg. 271

"as long as you keep breathing ..." –Olaf Bergmann, et al., *Adult Neurogenesis in Humans* (2015), https://www.ncbi.nlm.nih.gov/pmc/articles/PMC4484963/; Kirsty L. Spalding, et al., *Dynamics of hippocampal neurogenesis in adult humans* (2013), https://www.ncbi.nlm.nih.gov/pmc/articles/PMC4394608/; Peter S. Eriksson, et al., *Neurogenesis in the adult human hippocampus* (1998), https://www.nature.com/articles/nm1198_1313

Pages 37-38 –

"incorporate them into the cognitive networks of your brain ..." – Denise C. Park, et al., *The Impact of Sustained Engagement on Cognitive Function in Older Adults* (2014), https://www.ncbi.nlm.nih.gov/pmc/articles/PMC4154531/

"**series of studies demonstrating the brain building value of learning ...**" – Eleanor Maguire, et al., *Navigation-related structural change in the hippocampi of taxi drivers* (2000), https://www.ncbi.nlm.nih.gov/pubmed/10716738; *Navigation expertise and the human hippocampus: a structural brain imaging analysis* (2003), https://www.ncbi.nlm.nih.gov/pubmed/12699332; *London taxi drivers and bus drivers: a structural MRI and neuropsychological analysis* (2006), https://www.ncbi.nlm.nih.gov/pubmed/17024677

Map image of Central London excerpted from *Acquiring "the Knowledge"* paper, https://www.ncbi.nlm.nih.gov/pmc/articles/PMC3268356/figure/fig1/

Page 39 –

"**gave a battery of cognitive tests and scanned the brains ...**" – Katherine Woollett, et al., *Acquiring "the Knowledge" of London's Layout Drives Structural Brain Changes* (2011), https://www.ncbi.nlm.nih.gov/pmc/articles/PMC3268356/

"**Brain plasticity in the flesh!**" – *Healthy Brain, Happy Life*, supra, pg. 24

Page 40 –

"**one contrary study made headlines in 2018 ...**" – Shawn F. Sorrells, et al., *Human hippocampal neurogenesis drops sharply in children to undetectable levels in adults* (2018), https://www.nature.com/articles/nature25975.epdf

"**scientists from the pro-neurogenesis camp put it ...**" – Helen Shen, *Does the Adult Brain Really Grow New Neurons?* (2018), article reviewing the Sorrells study, https://www.scientificamerican.com/article/does-the-adult-brain-really-grow-new-neurons/

2019 Update: Emily Underwood, *New neurons for life? Old people can still make fresh brain cells, study finds*, sums up the issue: "The work 'provides clear, definitive evidence that neurogenesis persists throughout life,' says Paul Frankland, a neuroscientist at the Hospital for Sick Children in Toronto, Canada. 'For me, this puts the issue to bed.'" https://www.sciencemag.org/news/2019/03/new-neurons-life-old-people-can-still-make-fresh-brain-cells-study-finds; Moreno-Jimenez, EP, et al., *Adult hippocampal neurogenesis is abundant in neurologically healthy subjects and drops sharply in patients with Alzheimer's disease* (2019) https://www.nature.com/articles/s41591-019-0375-9

INDEXED REFERENCES

"**London cab driver series of studies provided a cautionary lesson ...**" – Katherine Woollett, et al., *Talent in the taxi: a model system for exploring expertise* (2009), https://www.ncbi.nlm.nih.gov/pubmed/19528024/

Page 41 –

"**another study specifically found ...**" – Jamie Talan, *White Matter Brain Changes Result from Reading Remediation* (2010), https://journals.lww.com/neurotodayonline/Fulltext/2010/01210/White_Matter_Brain_Changes_Result_from_Reading.9.aspx

"**a 2013 study of neural 'connectivity' ...**" – Gregory S. Berns, et al., *Short- and Long-Term Effects of a Novel on Connectivity in the Brain* (2013), https://www.liebertpub.com/doi/pdf/10.1089/brain.2013.0166

Page 42 –

"**concrete, action-related words and ideas ...**" – Cedric Galetzka, *The Story So Far: How Embodied Cognition Advances Our Understanding of Meaning-Making* (2017), https://www.ncbi.nlm.nih.gov/pmc/articles/PMC5534471/

"**Building your 'reading brain circuit' ...**" – this section briefly highlights research and observations from "Letter Three" on deep reading in *Reader, Come Home: The Reading Brain in a Digital World*, Maryanne Wolf (2018), pgs. 35-68

"**It is hardly coincidental ...**" – ibid., pg. 58

Page 43 –

"**The consistent strengthening of the connections ...**" – ibid., pg. 61

"**It synthesizes the text's content ...**" – ibid., pg. 62

Page 44 –

"**She poetically describes ...**" – ibid., pg. 68

Ch. 4 - Makes You a Better Leader

Page 45 –

"**A reader lives a thousand lives ...**" – George R.R. Martin, https://www.goodreads.com/quotes/615632-a-reader-lives-a-thousand-lives-before-he-dies-the

"**A 2015 report from the UK found ...**" – Josie Billington, et al., *Reading Between the Lines: the Benefits of Reading for Pleasure* (2015), pg. 8, http://www.letterpressproject.co.uk/media/file/The_Benefits_of_Reading_for_Pleasure.pdf

117

Page 46 –
"**Wolf cites a host of neuroscience research ...**" – *Reader, Come Home*, pgs. 42-53

"**The act of taking on the perspective and feelings ...**" – ibid., pg. 42

"**one study titled, 'Your Brain on Jane Austen,' ...**" – ibid., pg. 51

"**reminded me of a principle in ...**" – *Leading with the Heart: Successful Strategies for Basketball, Business, and Life*, Mike Krzyzewski (2000), pg. 101

Page 47
"**Another paper showed that reading fiction ...**" – *Reader, Come Home*, pg. 52

"**deep reading, especially fiction, contributes ...**" – ibid., pg. 52-53

Page 48 –
"**lists empathy as a core character attribute for leaders ...**" – *U.S. Army Field Manual on Leader Development*, FM 6-22 (2015), pg. 1-4, http://www.milsci.ucsb.edu/sites/secure.lsit.ucsb.edu.mili.d7/files/sitefiles/fm6_22.pdf

"**empathy makes better leaders ...**" – ibid., pg. 7-16

Page 49 –
"**brain scans ... reading fiction.**" – *Reader, Come Home*, pg. 52

"**indicators for leaders who display empathy ...**" – *U.S. Army Field Manual on Leader Development*, pg. 6-3

Page 50 –
"**In the workplace, empathy ...**" – Evan Sinar, et al., Development Dimensions International (DDI), *What's the Number 1 Leadership Skill for Overall Success?* (2016), press release with quote: https://www.ddiworld.com/global-offices/united-states/press-room/what-is-the-1-leadership-skill-for-overall-success; full report, *High-Resolution Leadership: A Synthesis of 15,000 Assessments into How Leaders Shape the Business Landscape*, section on empathy, "Is Empathy Boss?" with data chart and recommendations: https://www.ddiworld.com/hirezleadership/is-empathy-boss

"**dramatic change from the recent past ...**" – *Emotional Intelligence*, Daniel Goleman (1995), pg. 149

"**empathy as the fundamental 'people skill' ...**" – ibid., pg. 43

Page 51 –

"The leader must capture …" – *Learning to Lead: A Workbook on Becoming a Leader*, Warren Bennis and Joan Goldsmith (2003), pg. 122

"Bringing the necessity of empathy …" – Oren Harari, *The Leadership Secrets of Colin Powell* (2002), pgs. 199-213

"Powell says …" – ibid., pg. 211

Page 52 –

"to develop greater empathy as a leadership skill …" – Army Field Manual on Leader Dev., pg. 7-17, http://www.milsci.ucsb.edu/sites/secure.lsit.ucsb.edu.mili.d7/files/sitefiles/fm6_22.pdf

Ch. 5 - Makes You Smarter

Page 53 –

"The smartest people …" – Ageist editors, *Ageist Transformation: Reading* (2018), last accessed online 2/2/2019 via Internet Archive, https://web.archive.org/web/20190202154226/http://www.agei.st/reading

Pages 54-55 –

"In a 2001 report …" – Anne Cunningham, et al., *What Reading Does for the Mind*, http://www.csun.edu/~krowlands/Content/Academic_Resources/Reading/Useful Articles/Cunningham-What Reading Does for the Mind.pdf

Page 56 –

"a 2015 research review article …" – Gerd Kempermann, *Activity Dependency and Aging in the Regulation of Adult Neurogenesis* (2015), http://cshperspectives.cshlp.org/content/7/11/a018929.full

Page 57 –

"the sort of deep reading …" – see "Letter Three" on deep reading in Maryanne Wolf's book, *Reader, Come Home: The Reading Brain in a Digital World* (2018), pgs. 35-68

Page 58 –

"when people learn something, the wiring in their brains changes …" – John Medina, *Brain Rules* (2008), pg. 57, https://www.amazon.com/Brain-Rules-Updated-Expanded-Principles/dp/098326337X/

"The brain acts like a muscle ..." – ibid., pg. 58

"Impressive results from the Synapse Project ..." – Denise C. Park, et al., *The Impact of Sustained Engagement on Cognitive Function in Older Adults* (2014), https://www.ncbi.nlm.nih.gov/pmc/articles/PMC4154531/

Pages 59-60 –

"need for cognitive closure – our discomfort with ambiguity ..." – *Reading literary fiction can lead to better decision-making*, study finds (2013), no byline, http://nationalpost.com/afterword/reading-literary-fiction-can-lead-to-an-better-decision-making-study-finds

"The study notes other research ..." – Maja Djikic, *Opening the Closed Mind: The Effect of Exposure to Literature on the Need for Closure* (2013), https://www.tandfonline.com/doi/abs/10.1080/10400419.2013.783735

Ch. 6 - Helps You Live Longer

Page 61 –

"Do not read, as children do ..." – Gustave Flaubert, https://www.goodreads.com/quotes/2579-do-not-read-as-children-do-to-amuse-yourself-or

Page 62 –

"already talking about my next venture ..." – my current Old Dog Learning blogsite carries the tagline: Help, when you're feeling stuck. I describe my role as "Lead Guide Dog" and my vision for helping people (or teams) who find themselves in that "stuck" mode is summed up as, "Together we'll learn what you need to find your next path and get moving again with confidence and joy!" http://olddoglearning.com/

"the simple fact that we're living longer ..." – some of my thinking on how longevity can be celebrated and turned to our advantage can be found in my blog posts like, *How to apply Buddha's wisdom in the 21st century* and *Elderships: Filling the Experience Gaps in Your Organization*, https://olddoglearning.com/author/tom-collins/

"most babies born since 2000 ..." – Kaare Christensen, et al., *Ageing populations: the challenges ahead* (2009), https://www.ncbi.nlm.nih.gov/pmc/articles/PMC2810516/

Indexed References

"40 per cent chance of living for 150 years ..." – Angela Epstein, *Could your child live to be 150 years old?* (quoting leading population expert Dr. James Vaupel), http://www.dailymail.co.uk/health/article-129568/Could-child-live-150-years-old.html

"And then there's Google's 2013 investment ..." – mission quotes from the Calico Labs website, https://www.calicolabs.com/
In 2018, Calico began collaborating with a group at Penn, studying how medicines work, bring them to market faster, as well as "molecular clocks and circadian rhythm." When found, they want to deliver the "interventions that enable people to lead longer and healthier lives." https://www.calicolabs.com/news/2018/11/28/

Page 63 –

"According to a 2016 article ..." – Antonio Regalado, *Google's Long, Strange Life-Span Trip* (Dec 15, 2016), MIT Technology Review, https://www.technologyreview.com/s/603087/googles-long-strange-life-span-trip/

"Consider these U.S. age statistics ..." – 65+ fastest growing, *2010 Census Shows 65 and Older Population Growing Faster*, https://www.census.gov/newsroom/releases/archives/2010_census/cb11-cn192.html; 85+ expected to double, *Demographic Turning Points for the United States: Population Projections*, https://www.census.gov/content/dam/Census/library/publications/2018/demo/P25_1144.pdf; 100+ grew 44%, *Mortality Among Centenarians in the United States, 2000–2014*, https://www.cdc.gov/nchs/data/databriefs/db233.pdf

"Now, ask yourself why ..." – Art Swift, *Most U.S. Employed Adults Plan to Work Past Retirement Age*, Gallup Economy and Personal Finance Survey (2017), https://news.gallup.com/poll/210044/employed-adults-plan-work-past-retirement-age.aspx

Page 64 –

"offer you a short reading list ..." – Lynda Gratton and Andrew Scott, *The 100-Year Life: Living and Working in an Age of Longevity* (2017); Joseph F. Coughlin, *The Longevity Economy: Unlocking the World's Fastest-Growing, Most Misunderstood Market* (2017); Ilchi Lee, *I've Decided to Live 120 Years: The Ancient Secret to Longevity, Vitality, and Life Transformation* (2017); Chip Conley, *Wisdom@Work: The Making of a Modern Elder* (2018)

Page 65 –

"the concept of a few 'golden' years ..." – *The Longevity Economy*, ibid, pgs. 49-53

"combined pension and savings rate of around 9% ..." – *The 100-Year Life*, ibid, pgs. 46-48

"calculations for ... 20-35 years ..." – ibid., pgs. 54-59

"need to work into their 80s ..." – ibid., pg. 6

Page 66 –

"moving retirement ... to the middle ..." – Conley, *Wisdom@Work*, pgs. 154-155 (he adapts a metaphor from Mary Catherine Bateson comparing the added years of life to adding an atrium to a house, opting to put it in the middle)

Pages 67-69 –

"those aged 85+ report no health-based limitations ..." – David Lowsky, et al., *Heterogeneity in Healthy Aging* (2013), https://www.ncbi.nlm.nih.gov/pmc/articles/PMC4022100/

"benefits of reading books include a longer life ..." – Avni Bavishi, et al., *A Chapter a Day: association of book reading with longevity* (2016), https://www.ncbi.nlm.nih.gov/pmc/articles/PMC5105607/

Pages 69-70 –

"Reading as a life multiplier" – Steven Gambardella, *Seneca: Slowing Down Time* (2019) https://medium.com/lessons-from-history/seneca-slowing-down-time-badb389c3038; full text of Lucius Annaeus Seneca, *On The Shortness Of Life*, translated by Gareth D. Williams, https://archive.org/stream/SenecaOnTheShortnessOfLife/Seneca+on+the+Shortness+of+Life_djvu.txt, see paragraph tagged "(14.1)"

Ch. 7 - Print or Digital

Page 71 –

"When I read a manuscript ..." – Kerry Temple, *Out of the Office: The Science of Print*, https://magazine.nd.edu/news/out-of-the-office-the-science-of-print/

"how deep reading builds empathy ..." – *Reader, Come Home*, supra, pg. 52

INDEXED REFERENCES

Page 72 –

"reading books, especially print books, delivers ..." – Alison Flood, *Readers absorb less on Kindles than on paper, study finds* (2014), covering research by Anne Mangen, et al., https://www.theguardian.com/books/2014/aug/19/readers-absorb-less-kindles-paper-study-plot-ereader-digitisation

Page 73 –

"One theory on learning provides support ..." – Benedict Carey, *How We Learn: The Surprising Truth About When, Where, and Why It Happens* (2015), pg. 182-183, https://www.amazon.com/How-We-Learn-Surprising-Happens/dp/0812984293/

Page 75 –

Treble clef with middle-C image, adapted from public domain original via Wikipedia, https://en.wikipedia.org/wiki/Staff_(music)#/media/File:Piano_staff.png

Page 76 –

"Once you've got middle-C ..." – *How We Learn*, ibid., pg. 183

Page 77 –

Music notes adrift image, adapted from royalty free original via Pixabay.com, https://pixabay.com/en/notes-music-music-notes-clef-1417670/

"Other studies by lead author Ziming Liu ..." – described in *Reader, Come Home*, supra, pgs. 76-78

Page 78-80 –

"But she then describes her own experiment ..." – *Reader, Come Home*, supra, pgs. 96-104

Ch. 8 - Adopt Your Own Reading Plan

Page 81 –

"The more that you read ..." – Dr. Seuss, *I Can Read With My Eyes Shut!* (1978) https://www.goodreads.com/quotes/6806-the-more-that-you-read-the-more-things-you-will

Page 82 –

"The act of learning to read ..." – *Reader, Come Home*, ibid, pg. 2

123

"The reality is that each new reader ..." *Reader, Come Home*, ibid., pg. 107

Page 83 –

"Will the time-consuming, cognitively demanding deep-reading process ..." – ibid., pg. 106-107

"To prompt your thinking ..." – *Read More: 27 Ways To Get Reading This Year*, https://whywhathow.xyz/read-more-27-ways-to-get-reading/

Page 85-86 –

"Read, freely ... or at whatever price ..." – Marziah Karch, *How to Find and Download Public Domain Books From Google* (2017), https://www.lifewire.com/download-public-domain-books-google-1616290; Free ebooks - Project Gutenberg, http://www.gutenberg.org/; Kindle Unlimited, https://www.amazon.com/kindle-dbs/hz/signup/; BookLender unlimited plans, http://www.booklender.com/available_plans_unl.shtml

Page 87-88 –

"Post-It notes on the edges ..." – my original photos here and next page to illustrate my note taking methods

Page 88 –

"learning, and even earned a U. Penn. specialization certificate ..." – UC San Diego via Coursera, *Learning How to Learn: Powerful mental tools to help you master tough subjects*, https://www.coursera.org/learn/learning-how-to-learn; U Penn via Coursera, *Foundations of Positive Psychology Specialization*, five course sequence including a specialization project, https://www.coursera.org/specializations/positivepsychology

Page 89 –

"discovery-by-serendipity ..." – Tom Collins, *Global outsourcing sidenotes* (2004), http://knowledgeaforethought.blogs.com/knowledge_aforethought/2004/02/outsourcing_sid.html

"the planning-to-experience-serendipity side of PKM" – Tom Collins, *Accidental Discoveries* (2004), http://knowledgeaforethought.blogs.com/knowledge_aforethought/2004/07/accidental_disc.html

INDEXED REFERENCES

Ch. 9 - Take Action

Page 93 –

"**Adults are much more likely ...**" – Richard Pascale, *Surfing the Edge of Chaos: The Laws of Nature and the New Laws of Business* (2000) https://www.goodreads.com/quotes/6743830-adults-are-more-likely-to-act-their-way-into-a

"**In *The Story of the Human Body* ...**" – Daniel E. Lieberman, *The Story of the Human Body: Evolution, Health, and Disease* (2013), pgs. 329-343 https://www.amazon.com/Story-Human-Body-Evolution-Disease/dp/030774180X/

Page 95 –

"**I offer this image as a symbol for our movement ...**" – the "walking woman reading" silhouette symbol is adapted from two royalty free originals via Pixabay.com, https://pixabay.com/vectors/woman-books-school-reading-3971046/ and https://pixabay.com/vectors/woman-checking-mobile-smartphone-2803967/

"**Wolf's second experiment on herself ...**" – *Reader, Come Home*, ibid, pg. 101

Page 96 –

"**Lieberman closes out his story ...**" – *The Story of the Human Body*, ibid, pgs. 347-367

"**John Medina's Brain Rule #1 ...**" – *Brain Rules*, supra, pg. 7

"**subtitled 'Exercise Can Make You Smarter' ...**" – *Healthy Brain, Happy Life*, supra, pg. 135; 4-Minute Workout, Pt. I, pgs. 133-134; 4-Minute Workout, Pt. II, pgs. 160-161

Page 97 –

"**starting by emulating this employee benefit ...**" – Hailley Griffis, *Babies, books, and more: Buffer's 2018 in numbers*, https://open.buffer.com/2018-in-numbers/

Page 98 –

"**We must find the will to act ...**" – *Getting Unstuck: How Dead Ends Become New Paths*, Timothy Butler (2007), Pt. III, pg. 155 https://www.amazon.com/Getting-Unstuck-Dead-Become-Paths/dp/1422102254/

Page 99 –

"**Faulkner expressed it this way ...**" – William Faulkner https://www.goodreads.com/quotes/39009-read-read-read-read-everything----trash-classics-good-and

125

"**Toni Morrison is quoted ...**" – https://www.goodreads.com/quotes/321-if-there-s-a-book-that-you-want-to-read-but

Page 100 –

"**What I'm getting at is captured ...**" – J.D. Salinger, *The Catcher in the Rye* (1951) https://www.goodreads.com/quotes/1212910-what-really-knocks-me-out-is-a-book-that-when

Conclusion: As You Read

Page 101 –

"**As you read these words ...**" – Daniel Siegel, from *Mind*, supra, pg. 158

"**Recall from the Preface his proposal ...**" – ibid, pgs. 37, 155-156, and passim

Page 102 –

"**Patrick Sullivan proposes ...**" – *Deep Reading*, supra, pg.145

"**Louise Rosenblatt's image ...**" – ibid, pg. xiv

Page 103 –

"**Books are the plane ...**" – Anna Quindlen, *How Reading Changed My Life*, https://www.goodreads.com/quotes/2022-books-are-the-plane-and-the-train-and-the-road

"**I cannot remember the books I've read ...**" – Ralph Waldo Emerson, https://www.goodreads.com/quotes/37953-i-cannot-remember-the-books-i-ve-read-any-more-than

"**Reading furnishes the mind ...**" – John Locke, https://www.goodreads.com/quotes/50191-reading-furnishes-the-mind-only-with-materials-of-knowledge-it

"**No book is really worth reading at the age of ten ...**" – C.S. Lewis, https://www.goodreads.com/quotes/8293-no-book-is-really-worth-reading-at-the-age-of

"**Books are humanity ...**" – Barbara W. Tuchman, https://www.goodreads.com/quotes/155545-books-are-humanity-in-print

"**Think before you ...**" – Fran Lebowitz, *The Fran Lebowitz Reader* (1994) https://www.goodreads.com/quotes/56442-think-before-you-speak-read-before-you-think

Indexed References

Page 104 –

"**Fairy tales are more than true ...**" – Neil Gaiman, *Coraline* (2002) https://www.goodreads.com/quotes/17764-fairy-tales-are-more-than-true-not-because-they-tell

"**Sometimes, you read a book and it ...**" – John Green, *The Fault in Our Stars* (2012) https://www.goodreads.com/quotes/465988-sometimes-you-read-a-book-and-it-fills-you-with

"**If you don't have time to read ...**" – Stephen King, *On Writing: A Memoir of the Craft* (2000) https://www.goodreads.com/quotes/294383-can-i-be-blunt-on-this-subject-if-you-don-t

"**Start writing, no matter what. ...**" – Louis L'Amour https://www.goodreads.com/quotes/303969-start-writing-no-matter-what-the-water-does-not-flow

"**The best effect of any book is ...**" – Thomas Carlyle https://www.goodreads.com/quotes/21927-the-best-effect-of-any-book-is-that-it-excites

Page 105 –

"**What subliminity of mind ...**" – via Maria Popova on Brain Pickings, *Galileo on Why We Read and How Books Give us Superhuman Powers* (2016) https://www.brainpickings.org/2016/01/14/galileo-reading/; full text of *Dialogue Concerning the Two Chief World Systems*, Galileo Galilei (1632), translated by Stillman Drake, pg. 21 https://svetlogike.files.wordpress.com/2014/02/4-galileo-galilei-dialogue-concerning-the-two-chief-world-systems-1632-translated-by-drake-1953-abridged-by-s-e-sciortino.pdf

"**these words reach from within me ...**" – Daniel Siegel, from *Mind*, ibid, pg. 258

Page 106 –

"**a quote within a quote ...**" – Jessica Stillman, *Why You Should Surround Yourself With More Books Than You'll Ever Have Time to Read* (2017) https://www.inc.com/jessica-stillman/why-you-should-stop-feeling-bad-about-all-those-books-you-buy-dont-read.html

127

Intrigued by the opportunities for learning and the benefits of reading?

Let's work together!

I love helping individuals and teams break through obstacles that have them feeling stuck. Together we can learn what you need to find a path forward via our Professional Learning Partnerships.

If you're planning a event, we can start with a speaking engagement. I'm ready to present on many of the topics covered in *Read 'Em & Reap*, like:

- individual and organizational learning or reading plans (*Read 'Em & Reap*)
- effective multi-generational teams (*Engaging the Wisdom of All Ages*)
- applying the science of brain plasticity and adult neurogenesis (*Saving Baby Neurons*)

We also offer our Poplar Hill Asylum Retreats for intensive planning, exploration, or working sessions. And our focused Clarity Consultations are perfect for addressing well-defined questions (or identifying them).

To engage, or for bulk discounts on the book, contact me:

tom@OldDogLearning.com

www.ingramcontent.com/pod-product-compliance
Lightning Source LLC
Chambersburg PA
CBHW070546090426
42735CB00013B/3079